Living in His Presence

by
Brian Reddish

Living in His Presence
© 2020 by Brian Reddish
ISBN 978-1-9164868-6-7
Published by Caracal Books-United Kingdom
https://www.facebook.com/CaracalBooks/

All rights reserved. No part of this publication may be reproduced, stored in a retrieval system, or transmitted in any form or by any means—for example, electronic, photocopy, recording—without the prior written permission of the publisher. The only exception is brief quotations in printed reviews.

The internet addresses, email addresses, and phone numbers in this book are accurate at the time of publication.

Cover photo: www.shutterstock.com/Romolo Tavani

Unless otherwise indicated, all Scripture taken from the New King James Version®. Copyright © 1982 by Thomas Nelson. Used by permission. All rights reserved.

Historical Background and Introduction

The Jewish temple in Jerusalem was the place where animal sacrifices were carried out and worship according to the Law of Moses was followed faithfully. However, prior to this, sacrifices were carried out in the Tabernacle in the wilderness.

The Bible tells us that in the temple, a veil separated the Holy of Holies—the earthly dwelling place of God's presence—from the rest of the temple. This signified that man was separated from God by sin. He could not enter beyond the veil! Only the High Priest was permitted to pass beyond this veil once each year to enter into God's presence for all of Israel and make atonement for their sins. The veil was about four inches thick according to tradition! It was fashioned from blue, purple and scarlet material and fine twisted linen.

"You shall make a veil woven of blue, purple, and scarlet thread, and fine woven linen."
Exodus 26:31

The moment Jesus died upon the cross, something miraculous happened in the Temple!

"And when Jesus had cried out again in a loud voice, He gave up His spirit. At that moment the curtain of the temple was torn in two from top to bottom"
Matthew 27:50-51a

So, what do we make of this? What was the significance of the temple veil being torn in two when Jesus died? Above all, the tearing of the veil at the moment of Jesus' death dramatically symbolized that His sacrifice, the shedding of His own blood, was sufficient to forgive the sins of the whole world! It signified that now the way into the Holy of Holies was open for all people, both Jew and Gentile, for all time. When Jesus died, the veil was torn, and God moved out of that place never again to dwell in a temple made with hands.

> *"God, who made the world and everything in it, since He is Lord of heaven and earth, does not dwell in temples made with hands."*
> **Acts 17:24**

Jesus said that true worship is to be in Spirit and in Truth when He declared the following to the woman of Samaria—

> *"The hour is coming when you will neither on this mountain, nor in Jerusalem, worship the Father ... But the hour is coming, and now is, when the true worshipers will worship the Father in spirit and truth; for the Father is seeking such to worship Him.*
> *God is Spirit, and those who worship Him must worship in spirit and truth."*
> **John 4:21-24**

As long as the temple stood, it signified the continuation of the Old Covenant. We can now enter the Holy of Holies through Jesus. This is declared openly for all to see:

> *"Therefore, brethren, having boldness to enter the Holiest by the blood of Jesus, by a new and living way which He consecrated for us, through the veil, that is, His flesh, and having a High Priest over the house of God, let us draw near with a true heart in full assurance of faith..."*
> **Hebrews 10:19-22**

The things of the temple were shadows of what was to come, they all ultimately point us to Jesus Christ. The veil in the temple was a constant reminder that sin renders humanity unfit for the presence of God. The fact that the sin offering was offered annually and countless other sacrifices repeated frequently showed vividly that sin could not truly be atoned for or erased by mere animal sacrifices. Jesus Christ, through His death, has removed the barriers between God and man, and now we may approach Him with confidence and boldness.

> *"Seeing then that we have a great High Priest who has passed through the heavens, Jesus the Son of God, ... Let us therefore come boldly to the throne of grace, that we may obtain mercy and find grace to help in time of need."*
> **Hebrews 4:14-16**

This devotional book will lead us into a living relationship with God as a result of "entering in through the veil!" and is aptly called —

Living in His Presence!

iv

Day by Day Topical Index

PART 1 | *The Way into God's Presence*

Day 1 - Introduction—Beyond the Veil

Day 2 - "Therefore…"

Day 3 - Enter in Boldly!

Day 4 - God's Forgiveness

Day 5 - …By the Blood of Jesus

Day 6 - …By a New and Living Way

Day 7 - …By a New and Living Way (continued)

Day 8 - Having a High Priest over the House of God

Day 9 - Let Us Draw Near

Day 10 - With a True Heart

Day 11 - In Full Assurance of Faith

Day 12 - …**Having Our Hearts Sprinkled from an Evil Conscience** and Our Bodies Washed with Pure Water

Day 13 - …Having Our Hearts Sprinkled from an Evil Conscience **and Our Bodies Washed with Pure Water** (continued)

PART 2 | *Entering into God's Presence*

Day 14 - In Your Presence is Fullness of Joy

Day 15 - Come Before His Presence with Thanksgiving

Day 16 - Times of Desperation and Trouble!

Day 17 -   He that Comes to God…
Day 18 -   Asking of God
Day 19 -   The Holy Spirit Helps, Strengthens and Empowers
Day 20 -   Seek the Giver and Not Just the Gift!
Day 21 -   Abiding in Christ
Day 22 -   The Secret Place
Day 23 -   The Fear of the Lord
Day 24 -   The Secret Place—God Our Refuge
Day 25 -   The Secret Place—God Our Strength
Day 26 -   The Secret Place—Allowing God to Do His Work
Day 27 -   The Emmaus Road
Day 28 -   Counsel and Understanding

PART 3 | *Prayer Is the Battleground*

Day 29 -   Spiritual Warfare
Day 30 -   Spiritual Warfare—Who Is the Enemy?
Day 31 -   The Heavenly Places

PART 1

The Way into God's Presence

DAY 1

Introduction — Beyond the Veil

"...We have as an anchor of the soul, both sure and steadfast, and which enters the Presence behind the veil..."
Hebrews 6:19

The veil in the temple was torn from top to bottom at the moment Jesus died upon the cross. This is significant and is crucial to remember. It is God's removal of the Old Covenant and the establishing of the New Covenant! The very presence of the Veil in the Jewish Temple signified the barrier of sin between us and God. The tearing down of this Veil tells us the reverse is true — the barrier has been torn down.

It was God Himself Who tore down the curtain that separated man from God. This indicated that a new way was opened into the presence of God. If God opens up a door, then no man can close it. The significance of this is beyond measure. It is necessary to understand just why God tore down the curtain in the first place and what this really means. We will examine this more closely.

The days we are living in are called the days of God's Grace (or the Dispensation of Grace) and all because of this incredible occurrence the tearing of the curtain which clearly has opened up "The Holy of Holies." This signifies a new era of grace — but how does it do this?

Tradition tells us that the thickness of the Veil or curtain was the width of a man's hand, that is, about four inches thick. Its height was about thirty feet, the same as its width. The Veil was definitely meant to be a barrier to prevent entry as well as to conceal everything behind it. Behind the Veil, God's presence would abide high and lifted up. This area was known as the Holiest of All. The High Priest entered it once each year to ask for atonement of the nation's sins through the blood of the sacrifices and all the people would wait outside of the tabernacle. Were they in fear and trepidation waiting for Him to return, hoping that God would accept the offering? This background will help us see the significance of what Jesus has accomplished through His death and resurrection and why the veil was torn down.

When Jesus was crucified upon the cross and died, He became the sin offering to God! His own shed blood was to be the sacrifice for sin. After Jesus rose again from the dead, He went back into Heaven to His Father (The True Holy of Holies) as our Great High Priest, presenting Himself and His own shed blood as the sacrifice for the sins of the whole world! The resurrection of Jesus confirmed that His shed blood was sufficient to forgive all our sins!

"Now where there is remission (forgiveness) of these, (our sins) **there is no longer an offering for sin."**
Hebrews 10:18

This is the significance of the torn-down veil. This is what is meant by "God's Grace". Jesus has put away sin once and for all by the sacrifice of Himself through His own shed blood and provided for a new and living way into God's presence! Even eternity will not be long enough for us to fully grasp just what Jesus has accomplished at Calvary. Nevertheless, we can benefit from God's amazing love in sending His only Son to die for us. We simply have to receive Him ourselves as our Lord and Saviour.

As the Hymn writer said:

> *Give me a sight, O Saviour,*
> *Of Thy wondrous love to me,*
> *Of the love that brought Thee down to earth,*
> *To die on Calvary.*
>
> *Oh, make me understand it,*
> *Help me to take it in,*
> *What it meant to Thee, the Holy One,*
> *To bear away my sin.*
>
> **K. A. M. Kelly (1869-1942)**

It has often been said that "Grace" is God's unmerited favour. When you consider the fact that we were all enemies of God and "condemned sinners" lost as a result of the Fall, we realise that what Jesus did was entirely because of His love, grace and mercy. We did not deserve it! Now, in Him God receives us and forgives us. His sacrificial death, His shed blood has paid the price (ransom) for our sin.

Below are some of the things that God has done for those who will come to Him through His Son Jesus Christ by believing upon His Saving Grace and receiving Him as their new life:

- God has blessed us
- Accepted us
- Made us holy
- Made us without blame before Him in love
- Adopted us into His family as sons and daughters

- Redeemed us (i.e. paid the cost or ransom to buy us back through the blood of Christ)
- Forgiven us …!

Ephesians Chapter 1

The important thing to remember here is that it had nothing to do with man. As we begin our journey of meditations on entering into His presence "through the veil," one thing is important to keep in mind — the initiative was entirely God's. He accomplished it all through His Son Jesus Christ. He alone has made a way for us to freely enter directly into God's presence having removed the barrier of sin for us through His own blood.

The Bible puts it this way:

> *"…For by grace you have been saved through faith, and that not of yourselves; it is the gift of God, not of works, lest anyone should boast."*
> **Ephesians 2:8-9**

How do I freely come into God's presence? As already mentioned, the High Priest on the Day of Atonement was the only person to enter behind the veil with blood for his own sins and blood for the nation. How do I come to God and be received by Him? What must I do?

First, God calls everyone to come to Him through His Son Jesus Christ by being prepared to think completely differently about Him, ourselves and the purpose of our life (called repentance).

> *"…but now (God) commands all men everywhere to repent, because He has appointed a day on which He will judge the world in righteousness by the Man whom He has ordained. He has given assurance of this to all by raising Him from the dead."*
>
> **Acts 17:30-31**

Secondly, the Bible says each one of us must be "born again" of God's Holy Spirit and His Word. To be born again, therefore, means this — we must **repent** and **receive Christ** as our **Lord and Saviour**.

> *"Jesus answered and said to Nicodemus, "Most assuredly, I say to you, unless one is **born again**, He cannot see the Kingdom of God."*
>
> **John 3:3**

> *"…as many as received Him, (Jesus) to them He gave the right to become children of God, to those who believe in His name: who were born, not of blood, nor of the will of the flesh, nor of the will of man, but of God."*
>
> **John 1:12**

If you have never received Jesus personally and never thanked Him for dying for your sins, it is sufficient to prayerfully believe what the Bible here is teaching us to do in order to be sure you are saved from sin.

> *"For God so loved the world that He gave His only begotten Son, that whoever believes in Him should not perish but have everlasting life."*
>
> **John 3:16**

PRAYER

Thank you, Lord, that you have made a way possible for me to come to you and be forgiven through Your Son Jesus Christ. I understand that it has nothing to do with what I have done, but it is entirely by Your Grace alone I can be forgiven and saved.

Please forgive me for all my sins. I repent and choose to think completely differently from now on about Your Word, the Bible, and all that it tells me.

I understand that it is through the shed blood of Jesus Christ alone upon the cross that I am forgiven.

Lord, I give my life to you!

Help me from this day forward to trust you, obey you and follow you.

Amen

DAY 2

"Therefore…"

*"**Therefore,** brethren, having boldness to enter the Holiest by the blood of Jesus, by a new and living way which He consecrated for us, through the veil, that is, His flesh, and having a High Priest over the house of God, let us draw near with a true heart in full assurance of faith, having our hearts sprinkled from an evil conscience and our bodies washed with pure water."*
Hebrews 10:19-22

We are going to look at the above passage of Scripture in detail, day by day. It outlines the type of good attitudes we should have as we come into God's presence through Jesus Christ.

The opening word "therefore" suggests we need to look back to see what has been said before. To do this we will go back to the beginning of Hebrews chapter 10.

The book of Hebrews gives us great insight into the plans and purposes of God in His Son, Jesus Christ, and shows us what the blood of Jesus Christ has achieved for both God and man.

Here is the first verse of Hebrews Chapter 10:

"For the law, having a shadow of the good things to come, and not the very image of the things, can never with these same sacrifices, which they offer continually year by year, make those who approach perfect."
Hebrews 10:1

This reveals a negative—that the sacrifices of animals were limited in what they could achieve. This in turn shows us an expression of God's heart's desire for perfection and His dissatisfaction with the Old Covenant whose sacrifices could never take away sin. This is seen by the repeated emphasis upon the imperfect and incomplete sacrifices offered under the Old Covenant. God longed for a better way. The better way was the appearing of His Son Jesus Christ whom John the Baptist called "The Lamb of God". Jesus, the Lamb, come to take away sin, once and for all, by the offering of Himself.

> *"But in those sacrifices, there is a reminder of sins every year. For it is not possible that the blood of bulls and goats could take away sins. And every priest stands ministering daily and offering repeatedly the same sacrifices, which can never take away sins – But this Man, after He had offered one sacrifice for sins forever, sat down at the right hand of God"*
> **Hebrews 10:11-12**

We look next at verses 5-7.

This passage talks of the person of Jesus Christ Himself. It is actually quoting from Psalm 40 where Jesus had previously declared His intention to do God's will by becoming the sacrifice for all sin.

> *"Sacrifice and offering You did not desire,*
> *But a body You have prepared for Me.*
> *In burnt offerings and sacrifices for sin*
> *You had no pleasure.*

> *Then I said, 'Behold, I have come –*
> *In the volume of the book it is written of*
> *Me – To do Your will, O God.'"*
> **Hebrews 10:5-7**

In fact, if we turn to **Psalm 40**, we read further interesting information.

> *"Sacrifice and offering You did not desire;*
> ***My ears You have opened.***
> *Burnt offering and sin offering You did not require.*
> *Then I said, "Behold, I come;*
> *In the scroll of the book it is written of me.*
> ***I delight to do Your will, O my God,***
> ***And Your law is within my heart."***
> **Psalm 40:6-8**

These two additions, highlighted above, are extremely helpful and illuminating regarding the Person of Jesus Christ. We need to learn about Jesus as much as we possibly can from the Scriptures. Our knowledge of God, however, is only illuminated in our hearts by the Spirit of God so the more we meditate upon God's Word, the more this personal knowledge of God in the person of Jesus Christ can be imparted to our innermost being. This understanding of Who God is and what He is like helps us when we turn to God in prayer by realising Who it is we are seeking.

First, it says: ***"My ears You have opened."***

This literally means "You have dug or enlarged" which clearly points to an increased sense of hearing!

What does this tell us? First, that the attentive ear and obedient heart as opposed to formal rites constitute true worship. God required obedience, and Jesus accomplished this to perfection from a true heart of love and devotion to His Father's will. The importance of obedience to God was vividly revealed in the first book of Samuel when he rebuked King Saul for not obeying the Lord's command. Saul, instead of obeying God, refused to kill King Agag in battle. Further, Saul took the best of the spoils for himself and his men when he was told to destroy everything.

> *"But Saul and the people spared Agag and the best of the sheep, the oxen, the fatlings, the lambs, and all that was good, and were unwilling to utterly destroy them. But everything despised and worthless, that they utterly destroyed."*
>
> **1 Samuel 15:22**

Afterwards, when Saul was approached by Samuel, he said to Samuel by way of excuse that—

> *"…the people had spared the best of the sheep and the oxen, to sacrifice to the Lord Your God."*
>
> **1 Samuel 15:15**

…but Samuel's reply was

> *"Has the Lord as great delight in burnt offerings and sacrifices, as in obeying the voice of the Lord?*
> ***Behold, to obey is better than sacrifice,***
> *For rebellion is as the sin of witchcraft,*

*And stubbornness is as iniquity and idolatry.
Because you have rejected the word of the Lord,
He also has rejected you from being king."*
1 Samuel 15:22-23

Secondly, **"I delight to do Your will, O my God,"**

This verse tells us a lot more about the quality of our obedience to God and points to the manner and the way.

Jesus was willing to obey, by delighting to do God's will! So, whenever we seek God in prayer, we should remember that Jesus, Himself, delighted in obeying God and was willing to walk throughout His life choosing only to do God's will. This is the kind of person we are praying to and it goes without saying that to truly follow Jesus, is to go and do likewise.

If there is one hallmark difference between the New and Old Testament, it is this—love. God requires us to love Him and that alone will enable us to perform the kind of obedience that Jesus has exhibited. Nothing else will work!

The third passage of Hebrews chapter 10 that is important to us is this:

"This is the covenant that I will make with them after those days, says the Lord: I will put My laws into their hearts, and in their minds, I will write them," then He adds, *"Their sins and their lawless deeds I will remember no more." Now where there is remission of these, there is no longer an offering for sin."*
Hebrews 10:16-18

This New Covenant is mentioned in detail later, but essentially it is the obvious outcome now that Jesus has provided for forgiveness of sins through His blood.

> *"He (Jesus) takes away the first that He may establish the second."*
> **Hebrews 10:9**

This is wonderfully stated at the end of the passage when it says:

> *"Now where there is remission (forgiveness) of these (our sins), there is no longer an offering for sin."*

Question: What does it mean that there is no longer any need for further offerings for sin?

It means

> **…we are truly forgiven ALL OUR SIN!**

PRAYER

Thank you, Heavenly Father, that Jesus Christ, Your only Son, has purchased for me complete forgiveness for all my sins, and this was through the price He paid for me by His own shed blood.
I know I can never repay this! The one thing I can do is give you that which you ask of me –

> **… *to give You my heart!***

DAY 3

Enter in Boldly!

> *"Therefore, brethren, **having boldness** to enter the Holiest by the blood of Jesus, by a new and living way which He consecrated for us, through the veil, that is, His flesh, and having a High Priest over the house of God, let us draw near with a true heart in full assurance of faith, having our hearts sprinkled from an evil conscience and our bodies washed with pure water."*
>
> **Hebrews 10:19-22**

Having referred back to the previous section of Hebrews Chapter 10, we now proceed beyond the word **"therefore"** to see what follows on. It is very important to understand the first part of the chapter as it links us to the word "therefore," and consequently with all that follows. Here is a summary of yesterday's reading:

- The law was a shadow of things to come pointing to a future day when Jesus Himself would be the sacrifice for sin.
- God's desire was for a better remedy for sin.
- Jesus ushers in a New Covenant between God and man—in His own blood
- This one sacrifice was sufficient for all sin forever
- A key verse was:

> *"Now where there is remission (forgiveness) of these (our sins), there is no longer an offering for sin."*
>
> **Hebrews 10:18**

The next passage—**verses 19-22**—assumes several prerequisites for entering God's presence, and we shall focus on each of these separately.

To begin with, today's text says "**having boldness**" to enter into the Holiest. The use of the word "boldness" may seem daunting to some at first sight! For example, it may be that you have many things in your past that still affect you detrimentally. You may have had personal matters, which you now remember with regret and shame. You might think to yourself, *"How can I possibly come boldly to God when I feel the way I do, knowing all of the things that I have done in the past that I now deeply regret?"*

First of all, in such cases, God wants us to know that through the blood of Jesus we are forgiven of all our sins, weaknesses and past mistakes. Secondly, we are never to rely upon our feelings but rather we should always believe what God has done for us according to that which is written in His Word. True remorse leading to repentance is acceptable and indeed required by God, but such solemnity is quite different. Indeed, the Bible says that:

> *"...Godly sorrow produces repentance leading to salvation, not to be regretted; but the sorrow of the world produces death."*
> **2 Corinthians 7:10**

True repentance is one of joyous liberation from sin and not despair! It brings the joy of knowing sins forgiven and becoming a child of God washed and made clean in the blood of Jesus. It is the beginning of a new transforming, lifegiving power that will always continue to release us and set us free.

Essentially, coming boldly to God in this passage is all to do with our **confidence** in Him, having full realisation and appreciation of what He has done for each one of us. In fact, if you take another look at this verse, it says that we already "**have boldness.**"

What exactly is this boldness? What does the word mean?

The Greek word for boldness is *parrhesia* and means, to be outspoken or frank. Here, the implication in Hebrews is to be "confident. If we truly know and understand our salvation and all Jesus has accomplished for us (as stated in the previous verses of chapter 10) we shall definitely be confident. Our confidence will not be in ourselves or what we have done because that could be discouraging. Rather our confidence is entirely based upon what God has done for us through His Son Jesus Christ! He has achieved for us total forgiveness of all our sins through His own shed blood. So, the onus is not upon our own worthiness but upon His. If we believe and know this, then we can come boldly into God's presence knowing full well that Jesus will receive us and that there is no condemnation. You see, God does not deal with us anymore according to our past sinful life when we come to Him through Jesus, simply because He does not see our sin anymore! This is the amazing declaration:

> *"Their sins and their lawless deeds I will remember no more. Now where there is remission (forgiveness) of these (our sins), there is no longer an offering for sin."*
> **Hebrews 10:17-18**

This does not mean that we will be exempt from difficult times. Perhaps there will be times when we feel tempted and low. Life is like that. However, did you know that Jesus was also tempted and had to face difficulties? The good news is that He never once failed God or sinned. Because Jesus suffered and was tempted Himself, He understands what we are going through when we struggle. He's been there! Jesus died for us because He loves us and desires to save us from all the consequences of sin that we have experienced and all the troubled circumstances that can envelop our lives. When we suffer, He understands more than we might think.

God is for us ... not against us! He is our best and most reliable friend and desires us to really know for ourselves what great liberty and freedom He can give us as we put our trust in Him. That, of course, is why Jesus is called our "Saviour". He continues to save us throughout our entire life!

Finally, Jesus takes delight in being the one through whom we can receive all of God's blessings. He loves us and cares about us much more than we can ever possibly imagine!

PRAYER

Lord Jesus, I realise that there is so much for me to learn!

I choose to come to You and Your Word and read it for myself looking to You to help me understand.

Thank you that you are such a loving Person that calls me without condemning me!

"There is therefore no condemnation to those who are in Christ Jesus; who do not walk according to the flesh but according to the Spirit."
Romans 8:1

"Who shall separate us from the love of Christ? Shall tribulation, or distress, or persecution, or famine, or nakedness, or peril, or sword? As it is written

"For Your sake we are killed all day long; We are accounted as sheep for the slaughter."

Yet in all these things we are more than conquerors through Him who loved us. For I am persuaded that neither death nor life, nor angels nor principalities nor powers, nor things present nor things to come, nor height nor depth, nor any other created thing, shall be able to separate us from the love of God which is in Christ Jesus our Lord."
Romans 8:35-39

DAY 4

God's Forgiveness

> *"Now where there is remission (forgiveness) of these (our sins), there is no longer an offering for sin."*
> **Hebrews 10:18**

Today we shall look at God's forgiveness in detail.
As a result of believing upon the Lord Jesus Christ, we are totally forgiven all our sins.

> *"I write to you, little children, because your sins are forgiven you for His name's sake."*
> **John 2:12**

The opening verse taken from Hebrews 10:18 emphatically declares this fact:

> The repeated sacrifices made for sin under the Old Covenant could never take away sin but the one sacrifice and offering of Jesus upon the cross did. Therefore, because our sins are forgiven in Jesus, there is no longer any need for further sacrifices!

That is, **"there is no longer an offering for sin!"**

This truth is so tremendous that we need to look deeper. Unless I firmly believe and, more importantly, actually see for myself what God has done for me and on my behalf when the Scripture tells us that He has completely forgiven me, then I will probably never fully appreciate my salvation in Christ. In other words, I need to see for myself the cost to God of my salvation. After grasping this, my life can never be the same ever again!

Further, when we understand what God has done, we will learn more about the God Who did it. Actions and words reveal the person behind them — in all of us! The Bible says that Jesus is the express image of God's person therefore Jesus has revealed Who God is and what God is like! In other words, to understand God and know Him we need to focus upon Jesus.

"...He (Jesus) made the worlds; **who being the brightness of His glory (God the father) and the express image of His person***, and upholding all things by the word of His power, when He had by Himself purged our sins, sat down at the right hand of the Majesty on high..."*
Hebrews 1:1-3

The Greek word for "remission" or forgiveness is *aphesis* and comes from the word *aphiemi* which means:

> To send away; to release from bondage or imprisonment; dismissal; sending away, and forgiveness with the added quality of cancelling out all judgement, punishment, obligation and debt.[1]

Now, there are certain words that, whenever used in literature, are in reference to God only and no one else. For example, God's love in Greek is the word, *agape*. Similarly, the word forgiveness — *aphesis*, specifically refers to God's forgiveness.[1]

There was a time when Jesus spent many days in Capernaum. One day, whilst He was speaking at a certain house, a large crowd gathered to hear Him when an unusual thing happened.

Many gathered together, so that there was no longer room to receive them, not even near the door. And He preached the word to them.

Then they came to Him, bringing a paralytic who was carried by four men. And when they could not come near Him because of the crowd, they uncovered the roof where He was. So, when they had broken through, they let down the bed on which the paralytic was lying.

When Jesus saw their faith, He said to the paralytic, **"Son, your sins are forgiven you."**

And some of the scribes were sitting there and reasoning in their hearts, "Why does this Man speak blasphemies like this?

… **Who can forgive sins but God alone?"**

Mark 2:2-7

knew that this word was attributed to God only.[2] As they rightly said —

"Who can forgive sins but God alone?"

---

[1] *Strong's Concordance,* ©1980 by James Strong, Madison, NJ

[2] *Strong's Concordance,* ©1980 by James Strong, Madison, NJ

Indeed, the scribes were correct, but they did not know or believe that Jesus could possibly be God manifest in the flesh.

The full meaning and implication of the different aspects of "forgiveness," as shown above, are of utmost importance as they cover so many different scenarios in our lives. God's forgiveness brings:

"a release from bondage or imprisonment!"

Jesus, on one occasion, confronted the Pharisees regarding being in bondage to sin:

> *Jesus said to those Jews who believed Him, "If you abide in My word, you are My disciples indeed. And you shall know the truth, and the truth shall make you free."*
>
> *They answered Him, "We are Abraham's descendants, and have never been in bondage to anyone. How can You say, 'You will be made free'?"*
>
> *Jesus answered them, "Most assuredly, I say to you, whoever commits sin is a slave of sin."*
> **John 8:31-34**

God's forgiveness releases us and sets us free. Acknowledging the truth about our sinful lives and experiencing God's forgiveness is life-changing!

When I see the word "Dismissal," I imagine what it must be like standing in a court of law waiting for the verdict to be announced. The spokesperson of the jury is summoned by the judge:

"Have you reached your verdict?"

Words resound through the intense, electric atmosphere of the courtroom.

"Not guilty, Your Honour!"

The judge lifts his gavel and strikes the sound block intensifying the sound as he does so, then he speaks the words:

"Case dismissed!"

What a feeling that must be!

God, knowing we are all sinners has cancelled our debt through the blood of Jesus Christ and dismissed the case of the multitude of sins written against us. In other words, we are released and set free!

Clearly, some people will experience this courtroom drama more than others, but the fact is, all of us would have had to stand in condemnation before a Holy Judge with certain eternal judgment hanging over us were it not for Jesus. The case of sin brought against us has been annulled through Jesus and His shed blood!

Now, the Bible says:

> *"There is therefore now **no condemnation** to those who are in Christ Jesus, who do not walk according to the flesh, but according to the Spirit."*
> **Romans 8:1**

Can we truly appreciate that all judgment, punishment and debt have been removed and that we have been saved from a lost eternity?

True forgiveness has no "strings attached" including any obligation afterwards towards the forgiver. This is because God has given us freewill. We still have to make the right choices and decisions even as God's children! This requires total humility and submission to God putting Him first in everything.

Is it possible, therefore, for someone to be forgiven or be blessed by God in some wonderful way and then later on seemingly forget any obligation they ought to have towards God? Yes! Roots of selfishness can often override all spiritual demands upon us!

There was an occasion when ten lepers came to Jesus asking for mercy. They knew He could heal them. Jesus said to them:

> *"Go, show yourselves to the priests."*
> *And so, it was that as they went, they were cleansed.*
> *And one of them, when he saw that he was healed, returned, and with a loud voice glorified God and fell down on his face at His feet, giving Him thanks.*
> *So, Jesus answered and said, "Were there not ten cleansed? But where are the nine…?*
> **Luke 17:14-17**

What does this story teach us? It is even this sobering fact: though Jesus healed all ten lepers, it was left to the individual's free will to respond accordingly. It is exactly the same with God's grace and forgiveness. If I receive Christ as my Saviour, receiving forgiveness, and all that goes with it, will I, in response, return and offer my whole life to Him? Will I desire only to do His will, or will I go about life in my own way? In effect, will

I allow Jesus to be my Lord as well as my Saviour?

God's Word calls us to submit to God and follow Him, but ultimately it is our choice to do so. God never gives up on anyone, but He does require my cooperation and submission to Him.

THOUGHT & MEDITATION

*"**I beseech you** therefore, brethren, by the mercies of God, that you present your bodies a living sacrifice, holy, acceptable to God, which is your reasonable service...."*
Romans 12:1

"Jesus said to His disciples,

*"**If anyone desires to come after Me**, let him deny himself, and take up his cross, and follow Me. For whoever desires to save his life will lose it, but whoever loses his life for My sake will find it. For what profit is it to a man if he gains the whole world, and loses his own soul?"*
Matthew 16:24-26

PRAYERFUL SONG

When I survey the wondrous cross
On which the Prince of glory died,
My richest gain I count but loss,
And pour contempt on all my pride.

Forbid it, Lord, that I should boast,
Save in the death of Christ my God!
All the vain things that charm me most,
I sacrifice them to His blood.
            ...
Were the whole realm of nature mine,
That were an offering far too small;
Love so amazing, so divine,
Demands my soul, my life, my all.
                    Isaac Watts (1674-1748)

DAY 5

…By the Blood of Jesus

> *"Therefore, brethren, having boldness to enter the Holiest **by the blood of Jesus**, by a new and living way which He consecrated for us, through the veil, that is, His flesh, and having a High Priest over the house of God, let us draw near with a true heart in full assurance of faith, having our hearts sprinkled from an evil conscience and our bodies washed with pure water."*
> **Hebrews 10:19-22**

Many terms in the New Testament find their origin in the Old Testament Scriptures. The book of Hebrews, in particular, makes numerous references to the tabernacle, the offerings for sin and the priesthood, as well as the specific office of the High Priest.

The particular phrase we will look at today is:

"… to enter the Holiest by the Blood of Jesus"

To begin, it would be useful to take a brief look back at those things that were "figures of the true" in the Old Testament Tabernacle. This will help us appreciate what otherwise may sound like strange terminology.

The Tabernacle was a large portable tent that God commanded to be made while the people of Israel were wondering through the wilderness. The tabernacle consisted of two chambers, the Holy Place or Sanctuary and the Most Holy Place, Holy of Holies or Holiest of all. Entrance into each chamber was through a veil or large curtain. Certain people from the tribe of Levi were appointed by God as priests and they are known today as the Levitical Priesthood. Only a priest could enter the first chamber and perform tabernacle duties, but not without the shedding of blood through sacrifice. (In the book of Hebrews chapter 9, you can find detailed descriptions of what was inside these two chambers.) The High Priest was the only person to ever pass through the second veil into the Holiest of All or Most Holy Place, and this was performed once a year on the Day of Atonement when the sins of the whole nation were "atoned" for by the blood of sacrifice. This was a shadow of things to come pointing towards the future day when the eternal High Priest, Jesus Christ, would Himself be the sacrifice for the sins of the whole world and not just a nation!

John the Baptist has clearly shown this, through revelation from God when he publicly disclosed the identity of Jesus as He came to be baptised in the Jordan river —

> *The next day John (the Baptist) saw Jesus coming toward him, and said, "Behold!* **The Lamb of God who takes away the sin of the world!**
> **John 1:29**

> *"...but now, once at the end of the ages,* **He (Jesus) has appeared to put away sin by the sacrifice of Himself."**
> **Hebrews 9:26**

The writer of the book of Hebrews clearly wanted us to see and understand that just as the High priest of old entered the Holiest of All into the presence of God with the blood of sacrifice, we also come into the presence of God through our High Priest, Jesus in heaven (the true Holy of Holies). **"by the Blood of Jesus!"** This is the message of God's provision of a full salvation for the whole world through the atoning blood of Christ!

This terminology would be well understood by Jewish Christians, who were familiar with the Old Testament law that governed sacrifices. Now you can see and understand more about what it says in our daily Scripture when it tells us that we can enter The Holiest boldly **"by the blood of Jesus!"**. Jesus Himself as our High Priest, has gone before us and is seated at the right hand of God making intercession for us. As stated, we come to God through His blood.

> *...when He (Jesus) had by Himself purged our sins, sat down at the right hand of the Majesty on high...*
> **Hebrews 1:3**

Whenever we come to God, He sees Jesus Who Himself is the evidence of the blood He shed for us upon the cross. On this basis alone, we are accepted in the Beloved! Because God accepts the sacrifice of His Son, Jesus, He also accepts us as we come to Him through Jesus. This fact reassures us that His shed blood has truly atoned for all of our sins making this way possible! Not only has the blood of Christ covered our sins and provided for our forgiveness, it has totally removed them out of God's sight forever! The blood of Jesus has truly opened the door of God's grace to mankind as they come to God through His Son. It is a door that no man can close!

It is this background that helps us truly comprehend the significance of the blood of Christ as the only means of approaching God. **As we learn this, it is not difficult to understand why Jesus is the only way into God's presence.**

When we come in prayer to God, we can reflect upon the cost that was paid in order for us to do so! We should always be aware of this saving grace of God towards us. We should never come with pride or self-righteousness; we should humble ourselves and bow before the Majesty on High.

THOUGHT & MEDITATION

Give me a sight, O Saviour,
Of Thy wondrous love to me,
Of the love that brought Thee down to earth,
To die on Calvary…

Oh, make me understand it,
Help me to take it in,
What it meant to Thee, the Holy One,
To bear away my sin.

Katharine A. M. Kelly, 1869-1942

Jesus said:

"I am the WAY, the TRUTH and the Life; no one comes to the Father but through Me"

John 14:6

DAY 6

...By a New and Living Way

> *"Therefore, brethren, having boldness to enter the Holiest by the blood of Jesus, **by a new and living way** which He consecrated for us, through the veil, that is, His flesh, and having a High Priest over the house of God, let us draw near with a true heart in full assurance of faith, having our hearts sprinkled from an evil conscience and our bodies washed with pure water."*
> **Hebrews 10:19-22**

First God tore down the veil from top to bottom indicating, as previously mentioned on DAY 1, so that there was no longer any barrier of sin between God and man. We have shown in much detail previously how it is only by the blood of Jesus we can enter God's presence, be forgiven and received. There is no other way. If you were to ask the question — why did Jesus come to this earth? There is only one ultimate answer — to be the sacrifice for our sins:

> *"...but we see Jesus, who was made a little lower than the angels, for the suffering of death crowned with glory and honour, that He, by the grace of God, might taste death for everyone."*
> **Hebrews 2:9**

> *"Inasmuch then as the children have partaken of flesh and blood, He Himself likewise shared in the same, that through death He might destroy him who had the power of death, that is, the devil."*
>
> **Hebrews 2:14**

Further, Jesus declared Himself to be the only "Way" to the Father when He said;

> *"I am the way, the truth, and the life. No one comes to the Father except through Me."*
>
> **John 14:6**

To understand the implications of the "new and living way" we can simply focus upon the life and Person of Jesus. Literally, these words mean—*new or fresh, and living.* It is a new way because no human being had ever before entered into the heaven of heavens; Jesus in human nature was the first, opening the way to heaven for mankind to follow.

In following Jesus, we will be—

- Walking in God's **Way** fulfilling His will.

- Walking in the **Truth** according to God's written Word.

- Living a **Life** pleasing to God.

> *"He who says he abides in Him ought himself also to walk just as He walked."*
>
> **1 John 2:6**

A hallmark of the life of Jesus was to do the Father's will by living a life of obedience to God's Word. Jesus highlighted this as the way that pleases God. In other words, if we should choose to follow Jesus, then His life is the blueprint for our life too. His life is the only life which pleases the Father, and this was confirmed when Jesus was baptised in the River Jordan by John the Baptist.

> ...And suddenly a voice came from heaven, saying, "This is My beloved Son, in whom I am well pleased."
> **Matthew 3:16-17**

So, this "New and Living Way" mentioned in Hebrews 10:20, can be seen as the one and only Way into God's presence and into heaven itself. Not only this but the Way is also emulating the living Christ's example in our lifestyle.

JESUS… in Person…is this WAY!
JESUS …in Person…is the TRUTH!
JESUS… in Person…is the LIFE!

Remember, Jesus is the embodiment of everything that matters to God, and He is the hallmark of God's life for me!

PRAYER

I thank You, Father, that You sent Jesus to die for me.

Father, I choose this day to surrender my life to You and I declare —

"Not my will but Your will be done."

CALL & DEVOTION

Let us come and devote our entire life to following Jesus by entering the "New and Living Way" to the Father through Him, embracing His glorious and victorious life as our own.

DAY 7

...By a New and Living Way (continued)

The Reality!

The Way Jesus came into this world was to deny Himself and devote His life entirely to doing the will of the Father—this is the pathway for us when we are born again into God's Kingdom. His Way is to be our way. This was the path of life He took, and it is the same path we are called to take also.

> *"Christ also suffered for us, leaving **us an example, that you should follow His steps.**"*
> **1 Peter 2:21**

Here is the real challenge for every believer. Jesus said:

> *"If anyone desires to come after Me, let him deny himself, and take up his cross, and follow Me."*
> **Matthew 16:24**

What does this mean from a practical perspective? First of all, it doesn't mean denying ourselves through practising any form of asceticism. An ascetic deliberately suffers pain, abstains or becomes reclusive, thinking that this will lead to some form of higher holiness! Indeed, many world religions practise this in some form or another! Such a doctrine—"that a person can attain a high spiritual and moral state by practicing self-denial, self-mortification, and the like"—

is not the meaning of "denying oneself" as mentioned by Jesus.

Asceticism can never be true. It would undermine and contradict the all sufficient cleansing power of the Blood of the Lamb, which alone makes us holy and acceptable before God without works. Rather, it means we should put the interests of God's Kingdom first and foremost in our life above and beyond our own plans (denying ourselves in the way and manner the Lord Jesus did). We should renounce self-centred ambition even if it hurts. We must take up "our cross" such sacrifices will result in true joy and fulfilment experiencing the fullness of Kingdom Life upon earth!

Jesus confirmed this when He went on to say;

*"...For whoever desires to save his life will lose it, but whoever loses his life for My sake **will find it**..."*
Matthew 16:25

By yielding our whole life to the plans and purposes of God we find true Life! If we think we know better and seek to do "our own thing" with no input or guidance from God, we will forfeit and lose God's better life for us with all His plans and purposes. The truth is, God knows what is best for me—I don't! He, after all, created each one of us, and He knows what is in us! By seeking God's Kingdom first and foremost, I enter into God's blessings. He is the blueprint—I am to follow.

A Testimony

Not many years after I was married and our first child, Stephen, had been on the scene for two to three years, I went through a phase of applying for jobs outside London. Now, from the outward appearance, we were, I suppose, living in relative poverty in a two-roomed unfurnished flat. I say "relative" because our families and relatives were living in the East Midlands where property was cheaper in two- or three-bedroomed houses with all that goes with them. Our parents sometimes made their feelings known about "our predicament" as they perceived it to be, and this goaded us into considering our options.

We were attending a good church where they believed and preached the Bible. We were involved in children's work together and had good friends, but our living conditions were deemed below par and, further, Pauline was expecting our second baby. It is amazing how much advice you get when a baby is on the way! Living where we were seemed to be a problem to most other people. Many of the reasons and advice put to us were well intended and made a lot of sense but, in our hearts, we knew it had to be God's will for our lives—whatever we chose to do!

So, I was occupied in researching other jobs and attending interviews for a lectureship away from London. Upon the third attempt, I came across a job advert that seemed to be perfectly fitted for me. I rushed to request an application form and meticulously filled it in, sealed the envelope and placed a stamp upon it. It was ready to go. Before proceeding any further my wife and I prayed asking for God's will to be done. At this stage, I felt uneasy about everything! You see, I had reassured myself all along that if it was God's will, then I would get the job. but that argument was not working this time! Now I really liked this job — but it was not to be! I tore up the letter and threw it into the bin! As a result, I immediately had a witness from the Holy Spirit of His peace and joy! The experience was very real and there was no question about it — God's plans and purposes for us were right where we were — in our two-roomed furnished flat serving God and being taught His Word!

This situation was a testing time for me. It was only by choosing to "deny myself" putting the interests of God's Kingdom first and foremost in my life — above and beyond my own plans and ambitions — that I felt at peace. I practised then what I am preaching!

Guess what? My wife and I served God for forty years in London doing what we believe was His will. Needless to say, we were blessed as a result and would not have moved anywhere else or done anything else differently to what followed on from that decision — and to think I could have easily blown it!

Ironically, it has to be said that living in London was not the ideal choice for me, having been brought up in the Derbyshire countryside, and yet this was where we were to reside for a very long time! People would tell me so very often — "Oh! I would not live in London. It is far too busy for me!" Upon hearing such comments, usually when informing others where I lived, I simply smiled to myself knowing full well the bigger picture! As we used to sing:

What matters where on earth we dwell?
On mountain top or in the dell,
In cottage or in mansion fair,
Where Jesus is, 'tis Heaven there.

As it happens, we are retired and now living in the beautiful countryside of Oxfordshire! God is no man's debtor; His promises are true. Jesus said to seek first the Kingdom of God and His righteousness and all these things will be added to you. He did just that! I have proved God to be faithful to His Word! Amen!

AN OLD FAVOURITE SONG

I want God's way to be my way,
As I journey here below.
For there is no other highway
That a child of God should go.
Though the road be steep and rough,
If He leads me it's enough,
I want God's way to be my way every day.

DAY 8

Having a High Priest Over the House of God

> *"Therefore, brethren, having boldness to enter the Holiest by the blood of Jesus, by a new and living way which He consecrated for us, through the veil, that is, His flesh, and* **having a High Priest over the house of God***, let us draw near with a true heart in full assurance of faith, having our hearts sprinkled from an evil conscience and our bodies washed with pure water."*
> **Hebrews 10:19-22**

In looking at the tabernacle of old, we have already seen that it was the function of the High Priest to enter into the Most Holy Place once each year. Essentially, he was fulfilling the role of an intermediary or intercessor taking the blood of the sacrifice before God as an offering, first for his own sins and then for the sins of the whole nation.

Jesus, however, was both the sacrificial lamb and the sinless High Priest. After His death (the sacrifice for sin), Jesus (the High Priest) went into the true "Holy of Holies," that is, into Heaven itself to make intercession for us! Jesus presented Himself as the offering for the sins of the whole world through His own shed blood and not just the sins of a nation. His one offering for sin completely satisfied a Holy God, appeasing His righteous demand for judgment according to the law.

So, Jesus became the mediator of the New Covenant in His blood just as He had said to His disciples at the Last Supper:

> *He …took the cup after supper, saying,*
> *"This cup is **the new covenant in My blood**,*
> *which is shed for you."*
>
> **Luke 22:20**

Notice that it is a New Covenant in "His Blood." God has declared to the whole human race a promise, a bond, an agreement that we can come to Him by this new and living way. Yes, this is the essence of the New Covenant. It is God's agreement and promise that all those who will come to Him through the blood of Jesus He will receive and pardon. Jesus is to man, God's love, grace, mercy and truth!

The Bible gives us some very comforting and reassuring words when describing the qualities required by a High Priest and to understand them will help and encourage us in our prayers when coming to God.

- A High Priest had to have compassion on the people and be a merciful and faithful High Priest in things pertaining to God for His function was to make propitiation for the sins of the people.

- We read that Jesus understands our troubles very well! He humbled Himself and entered this world in poverty so that He can empathise with the heart and life of every person and reach them however desperate and poor.

> *"For you know the grace of our Lord Jesus Christ, that though He was rich, yet for your sakes He became poor, that you through His poverty might become rich."*
>
> **2 Corinthians 8:9**

- In life He was tempted in all points as we are and yet without sin! He is also able to save to the uttermost those who come to God through Him, since He always lives to make intercession for them.

- Further, God encourages us to come to Him. No one else can fulfil the role of intercessor between man and God like He can.

> *"All that the Father gives Me (Jesus) will come to Me, and the one who comes to Me I will by no means cast out."*
>
> **John 6:37**

The Story of Zacchaeus

I like the account in **Luke 19:1-10** of the tax collector called Zacchaeus—a man who wanted to see Jesus. The invitation of Jesus for all to come to Him certainly included an unscrupulous tax- collector! Very few people, if any would show any compassion to this man. He stole from them taking far more taxes than he should! Many would say this was not the man to be singled out and given special treatment and yet, out of a whole multitude in the crowd, this was the person Jesus called down from the sycamore tree and actually went to stay at his house!

> *"Then Jesus entered and passed through Jericho. Now behold, there was a man named Zacchaeus who was a chief tax collector, and he was rich. And he sought to see who Jesus was, but could not because of the crowd, for he was of short stature. So, he ran ahead and climbed up into a sycamore tree to see Him, for He was going to pass that way. And when Jesus came to the place, He looked up and saw him, and said to him, "Zacchaeus, make haste and come down, for today I must stay at your house." So, he made haste and came down, and received Him joyfully. But when they saw it, they all complained, saying, "He has gone to be a guest with a man who is a sinner."*
>
> *Then Zacchaeus stood and said to the Lord, "Look, Lord, I give half of my goods to the poor; and if I have taken anything from anyone by false accusation, I restore fourfold." And Jesus said to him, "Today salvation has come to this house, because he also is a son of Abraham; for the Son of Man has come to seek and to save that which was lost."*

Luke 19:1-10

Can we know for sure exactly what was in the heart of Zacchaeus to make him want to see Jesus? Jesus did! What we do know is this, Jesus accepted him in a non-judgmental way, just as he was. It was probably this very fact that turned the heart of Zacchaeus and led him to completely change his life and behaviour! To be spoken to and received by Jesus even though He knew Zacchaeus to be a cheat, did the trick for him!

It is always comforting to experience God's grace knowing full well that we are the guilty party and ought to be rebuked for our wrongdoing. Had it been any other person and not Jesus, speaking to Zacchaeus, he would have been treated very differently — that's for certain!

The grace and love of God is beyond our human comprehension but it's real and to receive it is to be changed forever! Jesus, our great High priest is indeed the best representative possible between God and man. He has a compassion that reaches to the inner soul bringing healing, deliverance and salvation to all who will receive Him joyfully.

> "Seeing then that we have a great High Priest who has passed through the heavens, Jesus the Son of God, let us hold fast our confession. For we do not have a High Priest who cannot sympathize with our weaknesses, but was in all points tempted as we are, yet without sin. **Let us therefore come**
> **boldly to the throne of grace,** that we may obtain mercy and find grace to help in time of need."
> **Hebrews 4:14-16**

PRAYER

Lord Jesus, I understand much more about Who You are and what You have achieved for me.

Forgive me whenever I have prayed in the past without true gratitude and reverence! I can only say I am grateful to have such a God and Saviour. You truly did die for me! You truly did give Your life for me that I might live!
I yield my life to You, Lord Jesus, seeking to obey Your Word and desiring to only do that which pleases You.

THOUGHT & MEDITATION

Reading the Word of God enables us — by the illuminating power of the Holy Spirit present within the heart of each believer — to "see" and understand the kind of person Jesus is. The Holy Spirit has come to reveal Jesus.

Let us come in prayer before the Throne of Grace that we may obtain help in time of need!

More importantly perhaps, let us express our love and devotion to our Saviour establishing and enriching a personal relationship with Him for it is only God's love that can keep a child of God through life's difficulties and turmoil.

The Giver is always greater than the gift; the one who helps is of more importance than the actual help received for we will often need help!

DAY 9

Let Us Draw Near

> *"Therefore, brethren, having boldness to enter the Holiest by the blood of Jesus, by a new and living way which He consecrated for us, through the veil, that is, His flesh, and having a High Priest over the house of God,* **let us draw near** *with a true heart in full assurance of faith, having our hearts sprinkled from an evil conscience and our bodies washed with pure water."*
> **Hebrews 10:19-22**

So often, God can be the last person we think of when facing a dilemma!

A Testimony

One day, when two of my children were very young, they were being mischievous, jumping up and down upon a bed. In those days, we lived in a double-bedsitting room and had temporarily vacated it and gone into the kitchen area. Suddenly, we heard a cry — my little daughter had fallen awkwardly. To this very day my wife and I do not know what, exactly, she hit her chin against, but the result was a severe gash on the side of it! Upon observing her state, my immediate reaction was to place my hand over the bleeding wound and call out to God in prayer, after which we immediately called for an ambulance. Needless to say, she needed stiches.

I was used to praying to God and drawing near to Him about most things, and the above response had been my instantaneous reaction.

God calls us to come to Him in prayer *all* the time! He knows how weak and vulnerable we can be and desires to strengthen us through our continually drawing near to Him. One moment all can be fine and then, suddenly, calamity can happen!

This very point, regarding receiving strength when in prayer, introduces one of the many benefits we obtain whenever we come and draw near to God.

> *"Draw near to God and He will draw near to you."*
> **James 4:8**

He strengthens our heart through having communion with Him. We get to know God as a real person! Simply coming to Him and abiding in His presence is sufficient. Problems fade into insignificance simply by being still before Him and committing everything to Him. Any remaining worry and sting of difficulty is quenched by gaining assurance and peace of mind through believing and knowing that He is in control. He establishes within me a reality of His omniscient power that assures that He cannot fail me! His Word becomes alive!

> *"If God is for us, who can be against us?"*
> **Romans 8:31**

> *"In quietness and confidence* [in God's Word] *shall be your strength."*
> **Isaiah 30:15**

The beauty of a personal relationship with God is that it *is personal*! It is real and, as the title of this book declares, we are meant to "Live in His Presence!"

In this book of daily devotions, we are discovering the amazing benefits found only in His presence! This personal communion with God is, I believe, the most important thing for our lives because it develops our love for God. Hence, we will confide closely with Him and learn to obey and trust Him as a consequence! God's love working in us provides the substance and the means to fulfil God's will and purposes. No amount of service or ardent commitment can ever be a substitute for this.

God requires His love to be the motive for everything we do!

> "…*speaking the truth in love, may grow up in all things into Him…*"
> **Ephesians 4:15**

> "*For in Christ Jesus neither circumcision nor uncircumcision avails anything, but **faith working through love**.*"
> **Galatians 5:6**

This is far more important to my spiritual well-being, peace and joy than anything else that I could possibly do for God! Therefore, it is our greatest priority to draw near to God both in prayer and keep His Word close to our hearts.

Drawing near to God is not entering a church building or any other place dedicated to Him. God no longer dwells in temples made with hands!

You can draw near to God wherever you happen to be. God is omnipresent and by His Holy Spirit, you can find Him wherever you are. If you call upon Him in faith and truth… He will be there! Remember what Jesus said to the woman of Samaria at the well:

> *"Jesus said to her, "Woman, believe Me, the hour is coming when you will neither on this mountain, nor in Jerusalem, worship the Father… But the hour is coming, and now is, when the true worshipers will worship the Father in spirit and truth; for the Father is seeking such to worship Him. God is Spirit, and those who worship Him must worship in spirit and truth."*
> **John 4:21-24**

Drawing Near to Jesus — The Story of the Blind Beggar

> *"Call to Me, and I will answer you and show you great and mighty things which you do not know."*
> **Jeremiah 33:3**

The word "call" in the above verse means:

"To cry out… to shout!"

Our story gives us an example of this in action! Do you remember the blind beggar who heard that Jesus was passing by in a crowd? He was named Bartimaeus, and he desperately wanted the attention of Jesus, so he drew near to Him and cried out saying:

"Son of David, have mercy on me!"

Even though many people in the crowd told him to be quiet, yet he cried out all the more!

What happened next describes the sort of attention that God is willing to give to the individual who really wants Him. The Bible says that:

Jesus stood still! (See Mark 10: 46-52)

Jesus then called for the man and asked him what he wanted. Bartimaeus said to Jesus:

> "*Rabboni*, (or My Great One) …
> …*that I may receive my sight!*"

Jesus told him his faith had made him well and to go on his way. However, Bartimaeus followed Jesus on the road not wishing to leave Him!

PRAYER

Thank You, Lord, that I can draw near to You at any time and in any place.
Thank You that You will always be there for me!

A VERSE FROM AN OLD SONG

Standing somewhere in the shadows you'll find Jesus.
He's the One Who always cares and understands.
Standing somewhere in the shadows you will find Him.
And you'll know Him by the nail prints in His hands

DAY 10

With a True Heart

> *"Therefore, brethren, having boldness to enter the Holiest by the blood of Jesus, by a new and living way which He consecrated for us, through the veil, that is, His flesh, and having a High Priest over the house of God, let us draw near **with a true heart** in full assurance of faith, having our hearts sprinkled from an evil conscience and our bodies washed with pure water."*
> **Hebrews 10:19-22**

The word "true" is a good word, and it describes what God is like. If I were true to someone or something, then surely, I would be all of the following:

Trustworthy, Reliable, Genuine, Honest, Faithful…

The list could go on! Being true is what we desire, above all else, in our relationships… is that not so! Well, God is the same. If you are His child, then you are in relationship with Him! He wants you to come to Him **"with a true heart"** to establish that relationship. Though it requires time just as with all relationships, the real state of our heart is always manifest because of who we are whether it be a truthful, open heart or otherwise. Right from the start, we must realise that God —

> *"requires truth in the inward parts!"*
> **Psalm 51:6**

God loves us to be true because He is true! Being true means God can trust us; He can depend upon us as someone who is reliable. Can God say that of me?

By being open and true, I am being real! So, remember, there is no one more reliable, trustworthy and true than God Himself. He "truly" loves us with an everlasting love, and He is faithful to keep His promises.

Our passage this morning says to draw near with a true **heart**! If our innermost being is involved as we approach God, then our thoughts and feelings are more likely to be sincere. Clearly, God thinks so otherwise He would not specify this as a requirement. A person speaking superficially or insincerely is uttering words, but they have no real substance because they are not coming from the heart! They can be casual or hasty words with no real depth. Man cannot see the heart—but God can! A superficial approach will never lead to the desired intimacy and personal relationship with God because God is Truth!

God knows our heart and our motive in coming to Him. He perceives all. In fact, the Bible says He knows our thoughts from afar! If we come to God with a true heart, this pleases Him. He always desires us to be open, frank and truthful about how we are feeling. Whether we are feeling good or bad is not the issue with God. He always desires us to come to Him just as we are to be open and tell Him the truth! He knows what the reality is—what the truth is!

"And there is no creature hidden from His sight, but all things are naked and open to the eyes of Him to whom we must give account."
Hebrews 4:13

He is gracious and merciful. It is far better to tell God how you really are in your life than to" beat around the bush" so to speak. Don't hold back from saying exactly what you are really feeling. You see, He already knows the truth about how we are anyway. When we tell Him the truth, I believe He respects it more than we think! To be honest and truthful with God is vital whenever we come into His presence.

On one occasion Jesus warned the people that they were not coming to Him sincerely in prayer. Actually, Jesus was quoting from the Old Testament when His people of old prayed in a similar artificial fashion.

Jesus said of them-

> *"These people draw near to Me with their mouth,*
> *And honour Me with their lips,*
> *But their heart is far from Me.*
> *And in vain they worship Me..."*
> **Matthew 15:8-9**

If anything, God's salvation in Christ appeals to the heart not the mind. God's Word and the Spirit seek to break down the deeply embedded throne of sin within. Therefore, God has chosen to reach us in His love through Christ. The law alone could never achieve what God desired—a heart of love for Him.

We vividly see a display of God's great love for us in the cross. A person who rejects the work of the cross rejects the very expression of God's heart.

> *"In this the love of God was manifested toward us, that God has sent His only begotten Son into the world... In this is love, not that we loved God, but that He loved us and sent His Son to be the propitiation for our sins."*
>
> **1 John 4:9-10**

God will have nothing less. His Son gave His all hanging naked upon a cross! What should our response be? It is this:

To hand over to God the reigns of our heart. Then we can truly begin fulfilling the requirement to—

"...draw near with a true heart..."

It is the work of the Holy Spirit alone that can lead us to that place of repentance, through God's love and grace. Christ can only come in when my heart opens up to let Him in and love is what breaks down the barrier of sin and pride in an arrogant but blind heart.

A Testimony

There was an occasion in our early years of marriage when we were visiting family. Sunday morning came along, and it proved awkward and difficult to take a stand, leave the house, and go to church all by ourselves. The family were not Christians and could not understand why we would wish to go to church. You see, we didn't always go to church!

As it happened, we had previously found a church in town that was similar to the one we were used to attending, so we chose to go anyway. To be honest, I wondered whether we should go. The atmosphere had grown tense, and I was feeling conspicuous and, as mentioned, very awkward! We both went anyway!

A hymn we sang during the *breaking of bread* service I will never forget, and it brought me to tears to think that I had nearly not bothered going to church that morning. I was so glad that I did!

It went like this…

**King of my life, I crown Thee now,
Thine shall the glory be;
Lest I forget Thy thorn-crowned brow,
Lead me to Calvary.**

*Lest I forget Gethsemane,
Lest I forget Thine agony;
Lest I forget Thy love for me,
Lead me to Calvary.*

Jennie E. Hussey, 1921

A MEDITATION UPON GOD'S WORD

"Behold, You desire truth in the inward parts..."
Psalm 51:6

"My Son, give me your heart!"
Proverbs 23:26

"For with the heart one believes unto righteousness, and with the mouth confession is made unto salvation."
Romans 10:10

PRAYER

O Lord! You know me well!

Forgive me whenever I am hasty in my thinking and speaking.

I come to You now knowing I need to spend much more time in Your presence and most importantly… to come before You with a true, open and honest heart keeping nothing from You.

I desire to put You first; no one has done more for me than You have, and nothing in this world is more important than You.

DAY 11

In Full Assurance of Faith

> *"Therefore, brethren, having boldness to enter the Holiest by the blood of Jesus, by a new and living way which He consecrated for us, through the veil, that is, His flesh, and having a High Priest over the house of God, let us draw near with a true heart **in full assurance of faith**, having our hearts sprinkled from an evil conscience and our bodies washed with pure water."*
>
> **Hebrews 10:19-22**

The **"full assurance of faith"** means unwavering confidence; (see "boldness" on Day 3) a fulness of faith in God which leaves no room for doubt. God has revealed Himself through our Redeemer—Jesus Christ—so that, in every way, He deserves our fullest confidence. No-one approaches God in an acceptable manner who does not come to Him **in full assurance of faith!** What parent would not expect their child to come to them without "the fullest of confidence in them?"

> *"But without faith it is impossible to please Him, for he who comes to God must believe that He is, and that He is a rewarder of those who diligently seek Him."*
>
> **Hebrews 11:6**

Jesus turned to the simple faith of little children to make a statement regarding the faith of a child. A little child trusts and believes unreservedly and unconditionally. It is this quality, found in small children, that I believe Jesus is looking for in each one of us — to have a trusting, childlike faith. So, whenever you consider your faith in God, remember a little child and the kind of attitude they display towards the one they know loves them!

As complex adults, we can so often shrink back at the prospect of having to display faith in God! Why is this? First, it is because we are indeed complex! We have a mind problem that children do not possess! We analyse, rationalise, try to work things out by our own reasoning but this is not trusting and believing in God. Sometimes we can look inwardly to ourselves and waver because of our own unworthiness and past record before coming to know the Lord then wonder whether God will hear our prayers! If this is the case, we will falter because we are gazing in the wrong direction — at ourselves instead of God's Word. Faith is not looking at ourselves and our own resources, it is looking towards God and His! This is why we are to truly see and understand all that God had done for us in His Son as revealed in Scripture.

God desires our faith to work by love. The Bible declares that our faith increases upon hearing and receiving the words of God which, by the Holy Spirit's illumination, enlighten us to trust and believe in Him. This is how it can work out in practice:

The more I look to God in accordance with His promises and prove Him for myself, the more I discover that He really does hear me and answer my prayers. This reality provides a basic steppingstone to become empowered to trust Him for bigger things. I become confident in God so that I approach Him with increasing assurance and faith.

In this way, a "little faith" can grow just like a seed when planted in the soil? Jesus said:

> "...*assuredly, I say to you, if you have faith as a mustard seed, you will say to this mountain, 'Move from here to there,' and it will move; and nothing will be impossible for you.*"
> **Matthew 17:20**

Faith that appears small or weak to us can still accomplish the humanly impossible. The "mountain" spoken of by Jesus is describing an obstacle, hindrance, or humanly insurmountable problem. God can deal with "mountains" through the faith of people committed to Him who accurately understand and know His power, will, purposes and provision for their lives. If we do not sow a seed, we cannot expect a plant! If we do not make our requests known to God in prayer, and look for an answer, how can we learn to trust Him and know Him?

We are always directed in the Bible to come to God in prayer and, as today's theme declares, we can be encouraged to do just that. Remember, God says we all have a measure of faith given to us —

> "...***God has dealt to each one a measure of faith.***"
> **Romans 12:3**

The next time a difficult situation or problem arises completely outside of our control, what shall we do? Will we fret about it, worry and get all stressed? No! We can immediately bring the matter to God in simple faith. We can seek His will about it, trusting Him for His help and guidance. God does not prevent us from having problems; He has, however, promised never to leave us or forsake us in them. This is why it is so essential to keep bringing our situations in life to Him every day. Sometimes, there are really difficult times but remember He desires to be with us during them.

So, what is my first port of call when faced with a problem? Let it always be turning to God in prayer! Sow a seed! Trust in God! Believe He will — one way or another — give you the best solution.

THOUGHT & MEDITATION

The Bible tells us how many people in the Old Testament days lived by faith but also, they died by faith not having received the promises. Having seen them afar off, they were assured of them, embraced them and confessed that they were strangers and pilgrims on the earth.

*Having **"full assurance of faith"** is not some wavering hope or faint belief in God. When given a promise by God, we are to be fully persuaded that the promise is true! Then embrace that promise and keep it in your heart no matter what.*

PRAYER

Lord, I come to You in faith believing.

Whatever the answers are to my problems, I believe You know what is best for me.

Help me, therefore, to put You first as my priority in life.

DAY 12

...Having Our Hearts Sprinkled from an Evil Conscience and Our Bodies Washed with Pure Water

> *"Therefore, brethren, having boldness to enter the Holiest by the blood of Jesus, by a new and living way which He consecrated for us, through the veil, that is, His flesh, and having a High Priest over the house of God, let us draw near with a true heart in full assurance of faith,* **having our hearts sprinkled from an evil conscience** *and our bodies washed with pure water."*
>
> **Hebrews 10:19-22**

This part of the verse in Hebrews 10 points to the two principle ways God uses for the process of our sanctification through the Spirit. Their origin is found in the Old Testament practices associated with the sprinkling of blood and the washing with pure water. In fact, they point back to the ministry in the tabernacle where appointed people, called Levites, went to do service in the Holy Place.

Before the priests could enter the Holy Place to do service and ministry, they first had to wash their hands and feet with water and be sprinkled by the blood of a sacrificial animal. This was to purify them from the contamination of the world. These rituals may be considered as a type pointing to our need today under the New Covenant for our daily sanctification. They remind us of the need for cleansing in our hearts both by the blood of Jesus and the washing of pure water by the Word of God (Ephesians 5:26).

The early Hebrew Christians knew of this terminology, and it helped them understand the requirements for following Christ.

> "...for Christ is the end of the law for righteousness to everyone who believes..."
> **Romans 10:4**

Jesus has ushered in the New Covenant in His own blood!

Today, we shall concentrate upon the first of the two, namely:

...having our hearts sprinkled from an evil conscience ...

Just as the priests of old were sprinkled with the blood for their purification, so we are able to be cleansed by the blood of Jesus continually.

> ... if we walk in the light as He is in the light, we have fellowship with one another, and **the blood of Jesus Christ His Son cleanses us from all sin.**
> **1 John 1:7**

The Bible says that even the consciousness of sin could never be remedied under the Old Covenant. In the Covenant, given to the people through Moses, every year there was a remembrance of sins. The blood of bulls and goats could never take away sin and so those sacrifices could never bring the remedy that God wanted, they merely provided temporary relief to man's guilt. Had perfection been possible in this way then there would have been no need for the sacrifices to continue. There would come a time when they could cease. Instead the same sacrifices needed to be made continually year after year and this would have gone on forever except—God had a plan made in eternity! Everything pointed to the future when God provided for a better way—the coming of Jesus, His own Son. In fact, the ritual ministerial offices of the priesthood, the tabernacle and sacrifices were symbolic of Heaven (Holy of Holies) and were in type referring to Jesus Christ Who was Himself, the sacrifice as well as the High Priest. Jesus Christ came into this world as an eternal priest to provide an eternal sacrifice for sin once and for all! Of Jesus's sacrifice, it says:

> *"…how much more shall the blood of Christ, who through the eternal Spirit offered Himself without spot to God,* **cleanse your conscience from dead works to serve the living God***?"*
> **Hebrews 9:14**

The shedding of the blood of Jesus provided a permanent sacrifice for sin and produced an enduring and better bond between God and man in the form of a covenant. (Day 5) We remember this every time we participate in the Lord's Supper. Jesus said at the last supper

> *"…This cup is the* **new covenant in My blood***, which is shed for you."*
> **Luke 22:20**

Jesus died and rose again then went into Heaven itself—the true "Holy of Holies!" God has declared (hence it is a covenant) that any person coming to Him through the blood of His Son (the condition) will be forgiven. This is the pinnacle of all the covenant! Just as the blood was sprinkled upon the priests every day for cleansing, we also can receive the cleansing of the blood of Christ every day.

As previously mentioned, if the priest had been defiled by the world, he could not come into the sanctuary of God without being sprinkled with blood first. This signified his need to be made pure. However, there were other times when the blood of sprinkling was used.

In the case of the Passover in Egypt, the blood signified a covering of protection. After the blood had been sprinkled upon the doorposts and lintel of each Hebrew dwelling, that household remained safe and untouched. When the Angel of Death saw the blood, it passed over that house!

During special gatherings, blood was sprinkled on the people and also the book of the law that outlined the covenant between God and His people. This signified the ratification or confirmation of the covenant between God and His people.

What does this blood of sprinkling mean in reality today? Well, it has a daily relevance to the believer who will inevitably feel the need—through their own conscience—to be cleansed from guilt and sin as a
result of the day's activities. Every day we can intentionally or unintentionally sin in thought, word or deed and as a consequence, we need to confess our sin and be cleansed as seen earlier in **1 John 1:7.** Images that our eyes observe and words our ears hear can defile our

mind even if we do nothing and say nothing! In such cases, the Scripture tells us that we can come to God, where Jesus sits at His right hand and receive cleansing.

> "...if we walk in the light as He is in the light, we have fellowship with one another, and **the blood of Jesus Christ His Son cleanses us from all sin."**
> **1 John 1:7**

> "...If we confess our sins, He is faithful and just to forgive us our sins and to **cleanse us from all unrighteousness**."
> **1 John 1:9**

This is God's provision for the daily cleansing of our hearts from sin and its guilt for, as it is written —

> "… sin shall not have dominion over you, for you are not under law but under grace."
> **Romans 6:14**

It is quite true to assert that the blood of Jesus Christ avails for sin forever!

Remember, as believers, we are all sinners saved by grace! God saved us while we were yet sinners! He didn't wait for us to be good enough — we would never have made it! First, as a sinner we had to come to God through repentance, and after receiving salvation we regularly need to come to Him for cleansing. Any person, the moment they repent before Christ, is completely saved from all sin through the washing of the blood of Jesus. However, we still have to live an overcoming life against the evil world, the flesh and the

Devil. This is why the Holy Spirit comes to sanctify us as we submit to
the Word of God and His leading.

It is often misunderstood that being born again by receiving Christ entails our freewill decision to submit to His Lordship! Without this there is no sanctification process and we will remain carnal in our thinking with little or no spiritual development!

The blood of Christ has ushered in a full Salvation of deliverance from all sin and all guilt; it released us from the effects and grip of sin. Yes! There is power in the blood of Jesus! True repentance leads us to real victory and freedom as we acknowledge that we have sinned, and we desire to walk differently. This is an essential part of our sanctification and maturity. We are being changed from glory unto glory; from victory unto victory by the power of the Holy Spirit within us and by the cleansing of the blood of Christ.

Jesus prayed to the Father saying:

"I do not pray that You should take them out of the world, but that You should keep them from the evil one. They are not of the world, just as I am not of the world."
John 17:15-16

So, let us "draw near with a true heart in full assurance of faith, **having our hearts sprinkled from an evil conscience!"**

LYRICS FROM A FAMOUS HYMN

Would you be free from the burden of sin?
There's power in the blood, power in the blood.
Would you o'er evil a victory win?
There's wonderful power in the blood.

There is power, power, wonder-working power
In the blood of the Lamb.
There is power, power, wonder-working power
In the precious blood of the Lamb.

Lewis E. Jones
Born: 8 February 1865, Yates City, Illinois, United States
Died: 1 September 1936

PRAYER

I thank You, Lord Jesus, for becoming the sacrifice for all my sin!

I understand that Your sacrifice alone – Your shed blood – presents me faultless and righteous before a Holy God.

You require me to submit to You daily and be washed and cleansed from sin.

I now realise that **I am not my own; I am bought with a price.** *I belong to You to do Your will.*

DAY 13

...Having Our Hearts Sprinkled from an Evil Conscience and Our Bodies Washed with Pure Water (continued)

> *"Therefore, brethren, having boldness to enter the Holiest by the blood of Jesus, by a new and living way which He consecrated for us, through the veil, that is, His flesh, and having a High Priest over the house of God, let us draw near with a true heart in full assurance of faith, having our hearts sprinkled from an evil conscience and **our bodies washed with pure water."***
> **Hebrews 10:19-22**

Clearly, the ceremonial requirement for the priests in the Tabernacle to wash their hands and feet with water also pointed to a spiritual counterpart in the New Testament. (Exodus 30:17-21)

Our bodies require being washed every day, especially our hands. All kinds of germs, and bacteria are picked up on our hands and some can be extremely harmful! For example, my wife and I were on a cruise ship when a virus broke out with hundreds of passengers affected. This virus was transmitted through touch so that staff were constantly wiping door handles and handrails! Anyone who contacted the sickness was confined to their cabins for 48 hours! The most important preventative measure was to wash our hands regularly with soap and hot water!

The Scripture today talks about our bodies being washed with "pure water." Pure water is not easily obtained but when water is thoroughly filtered it is very cleansing! Some years ago, we chose to have installed in our house a mains water filter system that removed about 99% of all stone and impurities from the water. We lived in a hard water region and felt it would be worth it. To wash in this soft pure water was nice but the truly amazing thing was that as the pure water passed through pipes, kettles, washing machines and dishwashers it cleansed away all existing lime-scale! Washing machines only required half of the quantity of liquid soap and dishwashers never required any softening salt tablets.

Pure water is special, it cleanses the body, so what does the text mean when it says our bodies are to be washed in "pure water?" Well, rather like the build-up of lime-scale in kettles, we become contaminated by being in the world and need to be washed and cleansed daily in God's "pure water!" In Ephesians it says:

"... that He (Jesus) might sanctify and cleanse her (the Church) with **the washing of water** *by the word..."*
Ephesians 5:6

In the east, it was common practice for a guest, upon entering a house, to have their feet washed by a servant. Having traversed dusty roads wearing just sandals, this entailed the necessity for daily washing of feet and Jesus performed this duty Himself in order to demonstrate the need for humility. He also stated that having bathed, they were clean except for their feet! In other words, the body is "clean", but feet need washing every time a person came into a house from outside.

Spiritually, each one of us need the cleansing of

the Word of God every day because we get "our feet" dirty too! There are things that will need to be cleansed, especially matters that deal with our conduct, character and walk with the Lord. The Word of God, energised by the Holy Spirit, is able to cleanse our way in this world sanctifying us in the process. Those adverse things that enter the mind—they occupy and distract us—do they not? As we allow the words of God to enter our minds, we can engage our thoughts upon them! The more we read the Word of God, the more the Holy Spirit can recall it to our remembrance and over-ride all other contrary thinking! The truth of God's Word makes us free! In this way, we will be purified in our minds and cleansed!

> "How can a young man cleanse his way? By taking heed according to Your Word."
>
> **Psalm 119:9**

In all of this, it is the power of the Holy Spirit that provides the washing and cleansing of the Word of God as well as imparting the ability to live a life pleasing to God; it cannot be achieved in our own strength; it works by God's grace alone. Therefore, it is as we choose to come to God's Word and apply it personally that we, in effect, allow the Holy Spirit to work His transforming, purifying power in our life. I must choose!

Our minds, in particular, need to be renewed and our character to be fashioned to be holy, like Christ. Therefore, we must yield ourselves to Him freely all the days of our life!

> *"I beseech you therefore, brethren, by the mercies of God, that you present your bodies a living sacrifice, holy, acceptable to God, which is your reasonable service. And do not be conformed to this world, but **be transformed by the renewing of your mind,** that you may prove what is that good and acceptable and perfect will of God."*
>
> **Romans 12:1-2**

Remember, the battle ground in every believer is the mind! The passage of Scripture above emphasises the need for our minds to be transformed into God's way of thinking. Let us therefore submit to Him and learn to walk in His perfect will for each of our lives yielding ourselves to His lordship.

THOUGHT & PRAYER

We need to think about what we are thinking about!

The Word of God and the Holy Spirit are inextricably bonded together, working in unison to sanctify us in order to change us to be like Jesus. Having accepted Jesus as Saviour and received His forgiveness, let us go on to know the Lord – as both Lord and Saviour by choosing and allowing God to perfect His work in us through obedience to His Word.

PART 2

Entering into God's Presence

DAY 14

In Your Presence is Fullness of Joy

"You will show me the path of life;
In Your presence is fullness of joy;
At Your right hand are pleasures for evermore!"
Psalm 16: 11

Having spent the first twelve days looking at—

"The Way into God's Presence"

we now move on to "entering into His presence" to discover what the Bible tells us—what to see, what to expect!

Upon thinking about this I immediately thought of the above verse in the Book of Psalms which declares that in His presence there is fullness of joy!

The first thing to see and appreciate is that God is a joyful Person! In a world that is full of trouble and pain we can easily by-pass this very fact by being consumed with all that is happening in the world and taking place around us or, more likely, we may be devoured by our own circumstances and problems which, in themselves, do not seem to encourage us to be full of joy! People can very often use the word "joy" for pleasure or happiness. Simply stated, happiness is tied to our circumstances while joy is not. Think of verses like James 1:2-3 which says:

"My brethren, count it all joy when you fall into various trials, knowing that the testing of your faith produces patience."
James 1:2-3

Another verse regards our Lord prior to His suffering!

> "…Who for the joy that was set before Him endured the cross…"
> **Hebrews 12:2**

These verses indicate that we can find **joy** in trials and suffering; this is only possible because joy comes from **gladness in the Lord** alone. Such gladness in the Lord can exist even in difficult circumstances! For example, in this verse we see that Jesus was about to suffer! Yet He saw the results of His sufferings that would await Him. His love for God's salvation being accomplished through Him, bringing many lost souls to Heaven, brought about gladness within Him! The following passage taken from the book of Isaiah is a favourite of mine as it depicts a foreknowledge of the sufferings of Christ and the results that entailed.

> "When You make His soul (JESUS) an offering for sin,
> He shall see His seed, He shall prolong His days,
> And the pleasure of the Lord shall prosper in His hand.
> He shall see the labour of His soul, and be satisfied.
> By His knowledge My righteous Servant shall justify many,
> For He shall bear their iniquities.
> Therefore, I will divide Him a portion with the great,
> And He shall divide the spoil with the strong,
> Because He poured out His soul unto death,
> And He was numbered with the transgressors,
> And He bore the sin of many,
> And made intercession for the transgressors."
> **Isaiah 53: 10-12**

The verse from Psalm 16:11 below personifies God's joy by pointing to a place—"at Your right hand!"

> *"In Your presence is fullness of joy;*
> *At Your right hand are pleasures for evermore!"*

Ask yourself, Who is seated at God's right hand, and the answer to that question will reveal the source of God's joy! It is Jesus Christ, the eternal Son of God Who, having been raised from the dead, is now alive and lives forever more.

> *"…when He (Jesus) had by Himself purged our sins, (He) sat down at the right hand of the Majesty on high…"*
> **Hebrews 1:3**

He is the Saviour of the world to all who come to God through Him. To God, the Father, this is the greatest event in the history of all creation because the door of His grace has been opened to all mankind through the blood of the Lamb! God simply loves and desires all men to be saved and come to a knowledge of the truth. His Son has provided the very means for this to happen! That's why there is joy in Heaven! This joy is unmeasurable!

The New Testament gives us glimpses of God's joy and the reasons for it. Remember the story of the talents? Well, those faithful servants with whom God is pleased, are invited to enter into His joy!

> *"Well done good and faithful servant…*
> **enter into the joy of your Lord"**
> **Matthew 25:23**

We need to realise that God desires us to share in His joy! In this verse, it talks of "entering into the joy of the Lord" at the time when we see Christ—yet Jesus also desired that our joy may be full on this earth as well!

> *"These things I have spoken to you, that* **My [Jesus] joy** *may remain in you, and that* **your joy** *may be full."*
>
> **John 15:11**

Further, the revelation of Jesus Christ by the Holy Spirit to God's children is described in 1 Peter 1:8:

> *"Though now you do not see Him, yet believing, you* **rejoice with joy inexpressible and full of glory***!"*

This is a work of the Holy Spirit whom Jesus said would come! The Holy Spirit alone gives us a taste of Heaven! If God the Holy Spirit dwells within us, then surely this means God's joy is manifested through us also! In Heaven, we will be immersed in and surrounded by a joyous atmosphere, but this is hardly the case in our surroundings while we dwell upon this earth! Jesus prayed knowing very well that God's people cannot see Him, yet He asked for us to have a full personal realisation and awareness of Who He is as well as being familiar with His presence.

This is only achieved by the work of the Holy Spirit in our daily lives. Religion with its adherence to ritual and ceremony can never produce what the Holy Spirit readily gives to a repentant unbeliever who suddenly finds that they have been saved and washed clean from sin through the cleansing of the blood of Jesus through receiving Him as their Lord and Saviour!

Is Jesus real in your life?
A song writer once declared —

"You ask me how I know He lives —
He lives within my heart!"

Jesus, leading up to the cross, saw ahead of Him the joy that would be released on finishing God's work that He had been sent to do. As terrible as the cross was going to be, we are all called to **look at the way in which Jesus Himself faced His death** as recorded in **Hebrews 12:2.**

*"Looking unto Jesus, the author and finisher of our faith, who, for the **joy** that was set before Him, endured the cross, despising the shame and has sat down at the right hand of the throne of God!"*

Now we can clearly see more of a picture of what Jesus is like. His attitude and forward thinking in this verse reveal what was the most important thing to Him.

Let us stop for a moment and ask ourselves —

"What is the most important thing to me?"

"Do I experience the fullness of God's joy in my life?"

Much will depend upon our relationship with Jesus Christ and what can consume us the most in our lives! Are we grateful for what God's Son has achieved for us? The Father is! Gratitude is a word fast disappearing from our dictionary but a thankful heart and appreciation towards Jesus Christ is required by God from all who would have the hope and expectancy of reaching heavens joyful shores!

THOUGHTS & MEDITATION

The Bible reveals a fullness of joy that is unspeakable and ever flowing like a fountain. We can only engage in this joy with the fullness of the Holy Spirit active in our lives, indeed we are commanded to be filled with the Spirit. This is a recurrent experience of continually being filled!

God's joy, together with a full realisation of what Jesus has achieved for us, is imparted to our innermost being through the living presence of God the Holy Spirit!

> "However, when He, the Spirit of truth, has come, He will guide you into all truth; for He will not speak on His own authority, but whatever He hears He will speak; and He will tell you things to come. He will glorify Me (Jesus), for He will take of what is Mine and declare it to you."
>
> **John 16:13-14**

PRAYER

O Lord! I come to change my priorities in life!
Though there is much trouble in this world, the fact is You have overcome it and defeated the enemy!
Fill me with Your Holy Spirit that I might daily experience Your joy and presence in my life. I seek to serve You and minister to others of Your glorious salvation!

DAY 15

Come Before His Presence with Thanksgiving

The Psalms tell us so much about how we should come into God's presence.

*Let us come before His presence with **thanksgiving**…*
Psalm 95:2

The word "thanksgiving" means both to give thanks and to praise. Interestingly, it is derived from the Hebrew word, *yadah* and this is derived from *yad* which means *hand*![3] It was the common practice and the natural response when thanking and praising God to lift up your hands or extend your hands—and it still is!

*"…I will lift up **my hands** in Your name."*
Psalm 63:4

The same word is used again in Psalm 100:4.

*Enter into His gates with **thanksgiving** and into His courts with Praise!*

Hence, thanksgiving and praise form a precedent when coming into God's presence. It is not associated with any particular denomination! To spontaneously lift up one's hands to the Lord with praise and thanksgiving is the declaration of the Bible and is a most appropriate way to bless the Lord with our whole heart. The Bible

---

[3] *Strong's Concordance,* ©1980 by James Strong, Madison, NJ

also tells us that God comes and dwells with us in our praises to Him!

> *"But You are holy, enthroned in the praises of Israel."*
> **Psalm 22:3**

This verse tells us that God is enthroned in our praises. Other translations state that God "inhabits" the praise of His people. We are most likely the real beneficiaries of this! God's glorious presence in our midst. God's approval and confirmation only serve to strengthen us with His might and power in the inner man as we praise Him.

In the New Testament the theme continues and the giving of thanks in all situations of life is declared to be the will of God for His children. The assertion is that, whatever our circumstances are—good or bad—we should always thank and praise our God not necessarily for the circumstances themselves because they could well be adverse, but because we can be assured that He will always be our helper in them. When we look at the facts of our forgiveness and salvation there is always reason to be grateful even in suffering and tribulations. When we look at the way Jesus secured eternal life for us through His death on the cross, there is always sufficient reason for gratitude.

> *"Rejoice always, pray without ceasing,* **in everything give thanks; for this is the will of God in Christ Jesus for you."**
> **1 Thessalonians 5:16-18**

This promise is re-enforced elsewhere. It goes without saying that we will always tend to turn to God in prayer during difficult times in our life. Indeed, we are told to come to Him with all our cares and burdens. The passage of Scripture below is relevant:

> *"Be anxious for nothing, but in everything by prayer and supplication, **with thanksgiving**, let your requests be made known to God; and the peace of God, which surpasses all understanding, will guard your hearts and minds through Christ Jesus."*
>
> **Philippians 4:6-7**

The "giving of thanks" is written into this passage in spite of the context of being anxious about a matter. Why is this? The answer is simple! Whatever our need is; whatever the problem and dilemma may be, God is able to help in the situation so that we can assert our faith by committing it to Him, giving thanks in advance!

God loves us to express this kind of trust and confidence in Him by faith and be sure He will act immediately when we do so by granting us peace of mind as we commit everything to Him. You see, our lives are truly meant to be that of "Living in His Presence" in all circumstances. Our strength comes from the Lord Himself. In this situation it is the peace of God that we benefit from in anxious times.

Oh, how we need to recognise that Jesus is there for us day and night! That He desires to help us in our personal lives if we will but allow Him to do so.

...It's called having a personal relationship with God!

Why is it that so often we only turn to the Lord at the last moment when all else fails? In doing so, we miss out on the most important aspect of our salvation—having personal fellowship and communion with God Himself.

Jesus once said:

> *"Come to Me, all you who labour and are heavy laden, and I will give you rest."*
> **Matthew 11:28**

A child of God who has been born of the Spirit and come to a full understanding of Who Jesus is has a door opened wide to enter into God's fullness of joy through the infilling and enabling of the Holy Spirit. It is God's joy that we share as we give Him thanks and praise. It is not a human joy that can be manufactured.

As stated previously, God's joy is not based upon our circumstances. When things are good, we can be happy and when they are not so good, we can be unhappy but not so with joy! Joy is a condition of the heart that has been set free! Even when outwardly all seems to be against us, we can be confident in this—God is faithful and never changes. He has promised to never leave or forsake us!

The Holy Spirit is the Spirit of Truth and when you come before God with a thankful heart trusting and believing in Him, He is going to keep close to you. Through all trials and temptations, He will be with you. The response from heaven will be a manifestation of the Holy Spirit's witness in your heart bringing with it a joy and assurance that God is with you!

> *"The Spirit Himself bears witness with our spirit that we are children of God…"*
> **Romans 8:16**

God is like that! He loves His people to trust Him in faith, because He is working out a plan in their life that is going to be better than they have ever known or conceived in their mind. Having made our requests known unto God, having committed all to Him, allow God to get on with it! If you keep faith and stay fervent in prayer, praise and thanksgiving, you will reap the benefits. Be patient and love Him for Who He is, then the problems will diminish as you focus upon Him. God is a God of salvation! He is also our Heavenly Father! He saves His people. He sanctifies His people. He teaches and corrects His people, and He loves His people!

Whilst joy is undoubtedly an eternal quality of God it is usually expressed in the Bible in the context of the goodness and lovingkindness of God towards mankind. We are literally partakers of His joy; it originates from God Himself and is infused within our innermost being by the Holy Spirit!

Whenever we come to God in prayer, let us first thank God for His son Jesus Christ and His salvation even when we are bringing urgent and pressing needs that are uppermost in our mind. God knows our needs before we ask. He can perform miracles, release us from burdening pressures and drive away the enemy of our souls! Praise and thanks to Him!

THOUGHT & MEDITATION

"When he (Jehoshaphat) had consulted with the people, he appointed those who should sing to the Lord, and who should praise the beauty of holiness, as they went out before the army and were saying:

> *"Praise the Lord,*
> *For His mercy endures forever."*

Now when they began to sing and to praise, the Lord set ambushes against the people of Ammon, Moab, and Mount Seir, who had come against Judah; and they were defeated."
2 Chronicles 20:21-22

As Stephen was being stoned to death for preaching and testifying of Jesus, the Bible says His face shone like that of an angel. He was filled with the Spirit and with joy upon seeing Christ actually standing up waiting to receive him in heaven!
Acts 7:54-60

DAY 16

Times of Desperation and Trouble!

> *"…in my haste, I said*
> *'I am cut off from before Your eyes'"*
> **Psalm 31:22**

I remember vividly a time when troubles seemed to surround us as a family at the beginning of our walk with the Lord. We mentioned our predicament to a lady who lived in the upstairs flat of our property; she startled and shocked us by inferring that:

> *"I thought Christians were not supposed to get so much sickness and trouble in their lives!"*

Needless to say, we were not too encouraged to hear this response!

When people ask, *"How are you?"* they rarely wish to hear the actual truth, especially if you are not well or you have a desperate situation! Have you ever been there? Have you ever suffered reproach in times of troubles when really you wanted comfort and understanding?

Well, King David of old did!

Psalm 31 is special for those who are really suffering, and today we shall spend time meditating on large portions of it.

What exactly were David's troubles?

> *Have mercy on me, O Lord, for I am in trouble;*
> *My eye wastes away with grief,*
> *Yes, my soul and my body!*

For my life is spent with grief,
And my years with sighing;
....
I am a reproach among all my enemies,
But especially among my neighbours,
And am repulsive to my acquaintances;
Those who see me outside flee from me.
I am forgotten like a dead man, out of mind;
I am like a broken vessel.
For I hear the slander of many;
Fear is on every side;
While they take counsel together against me,
They scheme to take away my life.
Psalm 31:9-13

The Word of God is truly TRUE! It does not withhold the bad portions but reveals all — both the good and the bad! Can we handle this! Can we manage the thought of being open and honest?

God has written down for us the words and sentiments of David expressed by the Spirit so that we may learn what God looks for in His people who call upon Him — even when the person is a prospective king!

David was not perfect; neither are we! Yet he unhesitatingly laid his case and situation before the Lord as he perceived it to be. Listed below are some of his complaints:

I am in trouble;
My life is spent with grief;
My strength fails;
I am a reproach among all my enemies – especially among my neighbours;
I am repulsive to my acquaintances;

Fear is on every side;
They scheme to take away my life.

Certainly, there were times in David's life when he was hunted down by those who wanted to kill him, including some of his close acquaintances. In particular, the current king of Israel, King Saul, and his soldiers sought to kill him. David hid in caves with no food or drink, yet he had supposedly been chosen by God to be the next king over Israel!

It appears that even David's neighbours and close friends abandoned him, perhaps fearing of reprisals from Saul should they seek to help him. He felt completely alone and rejected!

Have we ever felt the same? "Where is God?" We may have asked in sheer exasperation! "Why is all this happening to me?"

David's heart was open and frank before God and, in our privacy, there is nothing to stop us from being the same — if we are truly earnest and desperate. Now some people cannot do this very easily — if at all. Why? Because of pride! God is humble, so do not be surprised if upon occasions He humbles us so that in good time He may exalt us. The Bible says God resists the proud but gives grace to the humble.

Further, God is truth. Consequently, He is quite happy for us to truly tell Him how we feel. Have you ever noticed how people know exactly where they stand with you whenever you speak frankly with them?

David knew God in a personal way and realised that He was the only One to turn to. David could humble himself. He could not understand, however, that God would allow him to suffer. He could not comprehend that one minute he had been chosen as king and then all hell appeared to break loose around his life! However, in all of his dilemmas, David did not blame God! In fact, after getting much anguish of spirit "off his chest" David began to think about the Lord. Perhaps he contemplated all of the good times, the singing and praising God with his harp and the joy of His presence in the secret place.

Suddenly, David changed his tone of prayer to that of faith and trust:

> *But as for me, I trust in You, O Lord;*
> *I say, "You are my God."*
> **My times are in Your hand;**
> *Deliver me from the hand of my enemies,*
> *And from those who persecute me.*
> *Make Your face shine upon Your servant;*
> *Save me for Your mercies' sake.*
> *Do not let me be ashamed, O Lord, for I have called upon You;*
>
> **Psalm 31:14-17a**

David had previously uttered the words—

> *"Fear is on every side;*
> *They scheme to take away my life."*

...but now he says:

"My times are in Your hand."

In other words, *I shall not fear man who threatens my life. You control the length of my days; my times are in Your hands!*

Observe just how David is obtaining strength from the Lord! How? By focusing upon God and His truth and goodness and not upon his adverse circumstances. David ultimately knows this one thing (that we would do well to take heed of ourselves):

God is in control — not man!

The final tone of David's prayers and supplications are totally transformed into utter and complete victory! He now unselfishly begins to think of others who suffer and encourages them to also hope in the Lord.

> *Oh, how great is Your goodness,*
> *Which You have laid up for those who fear You,*
> *Which You have prepared for those who trust in You*
> *In the presence of the sons of men!*
> *You shall hide them in the secret place of Your presence*
> *From the plots of man;*
> *You shall keep them secretly in a pavilion*
> *From the strife of tongues.*
>
> *Blessed be the Lord,*
> *For He has shown me His marvellous kindness in a*
> *strong city! For I said in my haste,*
> *"I am cut off from before Your eyes";*
> *Nevertheless, You heard the voice of my supplications*
> *When I cried out to You.*
>
> *Oh, love the Lord, all you His saints!*
> *For the Lord preserves the faithful,*
> *And fully repays the proud person.*
> *Be of good courage,*

And He shall strengthen your heart,
All you who hope in the Lord.

Psalm 31:19-24

David, at one point, realised that he had uttered rash words in desperation when he had said to God:

"I said in my haste, I am cut off from before Your eyes"

…but, nevertheless, he then acknowledged how that God still heard him!

PRAYER & MEDITATION

Thank You, O Lord for Your Grace and mercy!
Sometimes You appear to take Your time in answering prayers.
Help me to pray more fervently and trust You – no matter how long it seems to take.
Help me to realise that You are working things out for me when You appear silent.
I know in my soul that You will never abandon me!

DAY 17

He that Comes to God…

> *But without faith it is impossible to please Him, for* **He that Comes to God** *must believe that He is, and that He is a Rewarder of those who diligently seek Him!*
> **Hebrews 11:6**

Nothing pleases God as much as a steadfast faith in all that He is and promises to do. Notice that "coming to God in faith believing that He is," is a direct command for the verse asserts that we *"must believe!"* The prerequisite 'to believe' reminds us of what we discussed earlier that we can have *"boldness"* or confidence to enter the Lord's presence freely because of all that Jesus' death on the cross accomplished for us. Without this prior understanding, we lack knowledge and will not appreciate our position in Christ before God. Similarly, today, we are to understand that in coming to God in prayer, we must appreciate and believe in the kind of God we are approaching namely that:

He is, and that He is a rewarder of those who diligently seek Him!

It is important, therefore, to believe in an almighty, all-powerful, miracle-working God Who is merciful and gracious to all who call upon Him in truth. In short, believing that *"He is"* able to do exceedingly abundantly above all we can ask or think! God has unlimited resources, and the good news is that He makes them available to His children.

Seeing that our opening passage talks of *faith* and that *it is impossible to please Him* without it, we shall look at how small, simple faith in God can grow.

When you plant a seed in the ground, there is some work to do beforehand. The soil must be prepared by being tilled and well manured with compost and nutrients. Similarly, the harvest it yields requires our work — to bring it in. But Who actually provides the harvest? By faith we trust and rely upon the sunshine and rain without which there is no harvest. God has an unlimited supply of "harvest blessings and provision" but we can so often forget to do our part and wonder why He doesn't answer our prayers! If you ask God to give you a good crop of potatoes, it goes without saying that you plant them first!

Now this parallel applies to all requests of faith made to God so that we need to be ready and willing to do our part whatever it is that God requires. Ask yourself,

Does God expect me to do anything?

One thing has already been accomplished once I have prayed about a matter in faith, I have planted a small seed. A small seed is good and not to be despised because this seed, having been planted will grow! My continued prayers will water it and God will answer according to His will bringing about a miracle in the making. This is how we establish a *seedtime and harvest* principle with God. (See Day 11: "In Full Assurance of Faith")

In times past, I have turned to God with a need, believing that He is able to meet that need, but so often,

I have expected God to do everything for me! This is not the law of seedtime and harvest!

To be honest, however, there have been times when I did not know what to do but pray and continue in prayer, believing. Upon such occasions, I have prayed about a matter until my faith has been able to leave it with God, believing He will take care of what I have committed to Him, always realising it had to be in His own sovereign way and time.

Jesus Himself prayed in the Garden saying:

> "O My Father, if this cup cannot pass away from Me unless I drink it, Your will be done."
> **Matthew 26:42**

It is so necessary to abide in God's presence daily so that we can receive a word from the Lord to wait upon Him regarding our request. If we establish a relationship with Him, He ministers to us by His Holy Spirit and can guide us in our praying so that we pray aright. The fact is, we do not know everything about a situation but— He does! God has a thousand ways to answer every prayer; we must be patient yielding our will to which of these choices God should use. It is not our prerogative to tell God what to do and the way He should do it!

God is also able to give us understanding over time regarding our prayer request so that through the Holy Spirit's illumination we see the situation quite differently to the way we did at the beginning. We see other ways the prayer could be answered in the light of God's counsel. This is wisdom when God imparts to us His course of action and way of seeing things so that the solution is not always what we thought was necessary!

There was a very traumatic occurrence in my life, when my teenage daughter was diagnosed with a scoliosis of the spine! Basically, she had severe backache and when bending over, her back would twist to one side. She was sent to a special Orthopaedic Hospital in central London for treatment.

Now this condition could only worsen as she grew older and then it would require her back to be broken and rods placed in for support! This was the normal procedure! Upon hearing this diagnosis, I felt stricken with anguish and dire concern about the whole matter and nothing could remedy it! I used to get down on my knees and cry to God time after time, day after day, and this went on for several weeks. I did not wish for my daughter's back to be broken! She was previously the healthiest of children—and then this!

Would God heal her spine? What could be done?

Whilst I was praying and crying out to God, I had to trust that He was in control. It was difficult but by trusting I knew God would do something. I was sure about this, but what exactly? I did not know!

During a church service, we were asked to split up into groups of four and pray for each other. I told the group about my daughter and asked them to pray for her. They prayed but then a Nigerian lady suggested she could form a group herself and they would fast and pray for my daughter! I felt so blessed by her proposal and she and her Christian friends spent much time in prayer and fasting. I was about to help organise things with her when she said, *"No Brian, you don't have to be there, we will do this and pray with fasting to God! You just leave it to us!"*

One day I received a phone call from my church. Apparently, an elderly, praying, lady member of the church had walked into the building having received a vision from the Lord where she had seen me praying before God! The Lord had instructed her to tell it to the church and that they should inform me not to worry as all would work out well! She did not know my name but recognised me in her vision as the man who had previously been preaching at the evening service a couple of weeks earlier. From this information, I was discovered to be the person in question. Upon receiving this assurance over the phone, I was considerably put at ease and my anguish of spirit subsided, but the situation was still there. I lived thereafter by faith for a long time!

Some six months, later I had to return to the hospital with my daughter to see whether the condition of her spine had worsened. My heart was tense as the consultant came towards us with the results of a fresh x-ray. I was very blessed and relieved to hear him say that the new x-ray showed no further worsening of the spine and that, if anything, it had improved!

This process continued for two more years until my daughter had reached the age when her spine was fully grown and then, having shown no further worsening of her scoliosis, she was discharged and told she could live a normal healthy life! God was gracious, and we had learned to walk and live by faith trusting in Him and His personal word to us.

To this day, my daughter has lived a normal life and was told she could carry on with her horse-riding which she loved!

GRATITUDE & THANKS TO GOD FOR HIS WORD

Trust in the Lord with all your heart
And lean not on your own understanding;
In all your ways acknowledge Him
And He shall direct your paths.

Proverbs 3:5-6

DAY 18

Asking of God

There are many Scriptures in the Bible that instruct us to "ask of God" through prayer. These cover a wide range of circumstances from receiving—*that our joy may be full*—to not receiving—*because we ask amiss!*

> "Until now you have asked nothing in My [Jesus] name. Ask, and you will receive, that your joy may be full."
> **John 16:24**

> "You ask and do not receive, because you ask amiss, that you may spend it on your pleasures."
> **James 4:3**

Jesus teaches us to be persistent in prayer along with a sense of earnestness and wholeheartedness. "Whatever you ask for in prayer," Jesus said, "believing… you shall receive!"

(See Matthew 21:22; Luke 11: 5-19; John 16: 23-24)

Primarily, our needs are spiritual, and God desires to infill and equip every believer with all spiritual blessing that belong to us in heavenly places in Christ Jesus. We are explicitly told this in the opening chapter of Ephesians where it says:

> *"Blessed be the God and Father of our Lord Jesus Christ who has blessed us with every*

spiritual blessing in the heavenly places in Christ Jesus."
Ephesians 1:3

Jesus encourages us to continually ask, seek and knock. (See Luke 11: 9-13) Finally, He makes the point that if imperfect human parents will meet the needs of their children how much more can we expect our heavenly Father to bless us with the best gift—the Holy Spirit?

Whilst our primary needs are spiritual, a proper relationship with God through the Holy Spirit is the firm ground for assurance that He will provide both spiritual and material needs.

"Seek first the Kingdom of God," said Jesus *"and all these things will be added to you."*
Matthew 6:33

At the very beginning of King Solomon's reign, after the death of his father King David, God spoke to him in a dream and said,

"Ask what I shall give you?"
1 Kings 3:5

How would you react if God said to you, "Ask of Me and I will give it you?"

I guess a young man may ask for several million pounds and a powerful, fast car!

An older person may also ask to be rich with a nice luxurious house as well!

Elderly people would ask differently; good, pain-free health would be very welcome to them having learned from experience that possessions come second place to having to live with continual pain!

In answer to the question posed to him by God, Solomon replied and declared that he was hardly experienced or qualified enough to rule over God's great people so he asked for an understanding heart to be able to judge them, discerning between good and evil.

This answer from Solomon pleased God, and because he did not ask for riches, God made him very rich. Because he did not ask for long life for himself, God promised him that if he kept His ways, just like his father had, He would also lengthen his days. Finally, of course, God made Solomon the wisest person, wiser than all before him and all who would ever come after him!

Interestingly, it says in the Bible:

> *"If any of you lacks wisdom, let him ask of God, who gives to all liberally…"*
> **James 1:5**

> *"But of Him you are in Christ Jesus, who became for us wisdom from God — and righteousness and sanctification and redemption…"*
> **1 Corinthians 1:30**

In contrast to the heavenly wisdom that produces an atmosphere of peace, those who would seek worldly wisdom and hanker for the things of the flesh to satisfy their selfishness — their prayers are not answered.

> *"Where do wars and fights come from among you? Do they not come from your desires for pleasure that war in your members?*

You lust and do not have.
You murder and covet and cannot obtain.
You fight and war.
Yet you do not have because you do not ask.
You ask and do not receive, because you ask amiss, that you may spend it on your pleasures."
James 4:1-3

Regarding praying for the sick, those who continually seek God by entering the Holy Place in prayer, will receive an awareness by the Holy Spirit of "how to pray" about a given matter. It is through this close communion with God that we receive His wisdom, understanding and insight relating to those things we pray about. His wisdom is far above and beyond all that we can naturally think and discern.

Whilst the Bible teaches that God is the healer of bodily sickness as well as spiritual, see below ...

"If you diligently heed the voice of the Lord Your God and do what is right in His sight, give ear to His commandments and keep all His statutes, I will put none of the diseases on you which I have brought on the Egyptians. ***For I am the Lord who heals you." (Jehovah-Rapha)***
Exodus 15:26

"Bless the Lord, O my soul;
And all that is within me, bless His holy name!
Bless the Lord, O my soul,
And forget not all His benefits:
Who forgives all your iniquities,
Who heals all your diseases."
Psalm 103:1-3

…it must be said that the way and manner God will choose to heal is ultimately sovereign to Him alone.

The two verses of Scripture above directly refer to physical healing apart from and separate to spiritual healing. God has declared this by His eternal name, *Jehovah-Rapha*, which literally means—*I am the Lord Who heals you*. So, make no mistake, it is Biblical to pray to God for physical healing as well as all other healing! As in all prayers, persevere with wisdom from God.

Finally, we need to ask and seek God for all of the many aspects of our life! The healthiest and most appropriate way to come with our requests to a Holy God is through the "fear of the Lord" as written in Proverbs 1: 7 —

"The fear of the Lord is the beginning of knowledge…"

This "fear" is not the "terror of a tyrant" but the kind of awe and respect which will promote obedience to Him Who is the wisest of all. Coming into God's presence, in the fear of the Lord, is the secret of obtaining genuine wisdom and guidance in our prayers.

PRAYER & MEDITATION

"Show me Your ways O Lord;
Teach me Your paths.
Lead me in Your truth and teach me,
For You are the God of my salvation
On You I wait all the day."

Psalm 25:4-5

"I will instruct you and teach you in the way you should go; I will guide you with My eye."

Psalm 32:8

DAY 19

The Holy Spirit Helps, Strengthens and Empowers

Do you desire God's presence to be real and active in your life, your prayer times and your worship times? Do you desire to speak boldly for the Lord? An important function of the Holy Spirit is to help us in all of these by imparting His power into our lives—plus an infinite number of other things too!

First, as a "born again" believer, having been born of God through our repentance and receiving the Word of God; having been born of the Holy Spirit of God through receiving Jesus Christ as our Lord and Saviour, God has now provided for each and every one of His children power to witness, and power to serve!

To enhance our understanding, we shall look at certain Scriptures regarding what we have become spiritually in Christ:

> *"And you **He made alive**, who were dead in trespasses and sins…*
> *… God, who is rich in mercy, because of His great love with which He loved us, even when we were dead in trespasses, **made us alive together with Christ**…and raised us up together, and **made us sit together in the heavenly places in Christ Jesus**…"*
> **Ephesians 2:1-6**

> *"Who hath delivered us from the power of darkness, and hath **translated us into the Kingdom of His dear Son**"*
> **Colossians 1:13 (KJV)**

This, then, is our position in Christ!

One of the difficulties we all have is that we cannot "see" the things that are spiritual! Consequently, we can go through our life not receiving these spiritual benefits. Like with our salvation, our eternal hope for the future, our faith in Christ, we live by faith in God's Word. Through reading this book and coming to God in prayer, we have already established a knowledge of His presence in our daily lives. This is spiritual because we cannot see God and yet we can experience His presence and have assurance that He is with us. This is all part of our "born again" experience having been born of the Spirit. There is much more!

Practically speaking, we are now meant to live and walk in the Word of God and the Spirit of God. We are meant to be guided and taught by Him in all things. It does not take much convincing, having read what the Bible says we have become in Christ, to realise that the Holy Spirit should play a major role in our lives! However, as true as this is, I do not benefit from the position God has placed me in spiritually without giving my whole life to Him unless I surrender all my plans and ambitions to do His purposes. If God reigns upon the throne of my heart, I am able to enter into all the works He has planned for me to do from the foundation of the world!

Let us therefore take up the challenge God offers us by:

- Learning and knowing the Word of God and obeying it
- Seeking God for the reality of His presence, power and might in my life through the working of the Holy Spirit

It will not be a surprise when we come to consider "prayer or worship," that the Holy Spirit is there to lead the way. Our part is to recognise this and depend upon the Spirit wherever the Word of God directs us to do so.

First, the Holy Spirit desires to be active with us in our praying. So often when we pray, we can find it difficult to know what to pray for or how to pray. Sometimes we are not able to put into words the deepest thoughts of our heart's desires. We do not know how to express them. This is when the Spirit can come alongside us and help us!

> *"Likewise, the Spirit also helps in our weaknesses. For we do not know what we should pray for as we ought, but the Spirit Himself makes intercession for us with groanings which cannot be uttered."*
> **Romans 8:26**

Further, the Bible talks about "praying in the Spirit."

> *"But you, beloved, building yourselves up on your most holy faith, **praying in the Holy Spirit**..."*
> **Jude 20**

> *"...praying always with all prayer and supplication in the Spirit..."*
> **Ephesians 6:18**

"Praying in the Spirit" can be considered in conjunction with "speaking in tongues." The latter is both a gift used within the church but also a spiritual means of enhancing private devotion in prayer. In both cases, it gives personal edification enabling the Spirit to bring "down" the reality of God's presence to a new level in our innermost being and experience.

All other gifts of the Holy Spirit were in evidence during the Old Testament times, in some shape or form but "speaking with tongues", as the Holy Spirit gives utterance, is the unique spiritual gift identified with the church of Jesus Christ and it is mentioned by Jesus Himself:

> "And these signs will follow those who believe:
> In My Name they will cast out demons;
> **They will speak with new tongues..."**
> **Mark 16:17**

Jesus told us that the Holy Spirit is also our Helper or Comforter (*parakletos*) Who draws alongside. He is like a personal counsellor and guide Who is always with us! Whenever we engage in God's Word, prayer and praise, He particularly manifests Himself bearing witness to the truth in us and continually granting us that personal subjective assurance that we are the children of God.

> "The Spirit Himself bears witness with our spirit that we are children of God..."
> **Romans 8:16**

The Bible talks of "being filled with the Spirit."

> *"...be filled with the Spirit, speaking to one another in psalms and hymns and spiritual songs, singing and making melody in your heart to the Lord..."*
> **Ephesians 5:18-19**

Clearly, in heaven they praise and worship God! It follows that the Holy Spirit will seek to enable God's people to do likewise but notice that here, it is a result of "being filled with the Spirit." The Holy Spirit wants to be there in our praises! In everything, He will point us to glorify Jesus! Why not allow Him to lead you whenever there is praise and worship to God? The Bible says-

> *"Open your mouth wide and I will fill it!"*
> **Psalm 81:10**

Being "filled with the Spirit" in this context is not referring to human, exuberant utterances of praise though it certainly can involve them! It is clearly referring to the Holy Spirits involvement in our singing otherwise why "be filled with the Spirit?" Why not something else such as be "filled with joy?"

The Bible says God inhabits or is enthroned in the praises of His people (Psalm 22:3) (literally, comes to dwell and sets up His throne)! In other words, when we really praise the Lord Jesus from our hearts it creates the opportunity for the power and presence of God to be manifested!

In the Old Testament, when singers were appointed to praise the Lord whilst marching into battle, the Bible says the Lord came down and fought against their enemies! Praise brings victory — there is no question about it!

The text leads us to ask ourselves whenever singing songs and hymns, are we singing and —

"making melody in our hearts to the Lord?"

The fact that it mentions the "heart" at all suggests that our affections from the expressions of our innermost hearts should also go along with the words we are singing.

Additionally, being "filled with the Spirit" is not a "one-off" experience but a command that is in the present tense. The passage actually means to be continuously filled with the Spirit. This is not surprising since anything and everything we do for God each day must be done through the unction and energy of the Holy Spirit at all times if it is to be effective! It is like the "Higher" reaching down to lift the "lower" drawing us into ultimate communion.

My Personal Experience

I remember the time when I first came to believe in the Lord. It was in a small church hall where I received and experienced the reality of God and His Word, which changed me forever. However, I distinctly remember hearing people pray out aloud in the meetings, thanking and praising God but I was too afraid to do so myself. I desired to receive from God all that was going for me in the Scriptures.

The church was one of the original Bible-based Pentecostal churches, so I naturally heard about baptism in the Holy Spirit and the way this gave the believer power to witness and therefore, to speak out aloud! I decided to do whatever God's Word commanded me to do and very soon, I asked to be baptised in water by full immersion as a testimony that I had given my life to serving and following God.

I knew that after obeying this command to be baptised, I could then ask God in full confidence to baptise me in the Holy Spirit. This was my reasoning in the matter, and I did not know much of God's Word at that time but what I did know, I eagerly acted upon.

I have to say that I was young in the faith and knew nothing of the differing opinions in the Christian world regarding the baptism in the Holy Spirit and, for that matter, baptism in water. For this, I thank God!

So it was, that after being baptised in water I soon heard of a meeting back in London where they would specifically pray at the end for people to be baptised in the Holy Spirit. I went to that meeting fully expecting God to fulfil His Word in my life. Nothing sensational occurred but I firmly believed I had received it by faith and then looked to God to help me manifest the power of His Spirit within me!

Several weeks later, it happened. Sitting in the front row in a prayer meeting with a good forty or so people present, I felt a move in my spirit to speak out loud to God but I held back and hesitated not being sure whether this prompting was from God or of my own imagination. I did not wish to appear stupid! The pastor, who was convening the meeting, stood right in front of me and must have discerned something was happening inside the young man in front of him! He knew me well and bent and whispered in my ear—

"Do not be afraid Brian… speak out!"

Instantly, I was no longer afraid! I spoke out, very loudly, a message in tongues, for the very first time. A flooding of the Holy Spirit filled my being and afterwards the pastor gave an interpretation!

It was after this experience that I became reassured that God was real and true to His Word! I became confident and bold in my attitude with God! Needless to say, I was no longer afraid to speak or pray in public ever again! I now knew that God was with me! I just had to be bold, without self-consciousness or fear and step out in faith. I also realised that there was a spiritual world out there and with God's help I could be active in it!

> *"For God has not given us a spirit of fear, but of power and love and of a sound mind."*
> **2 Timothy 1:7**

PRAYER

Lord Jesus, fill me with the Holy Spirit so that I might have Your power to be Your witness speaking out for You with boldness and sharing the Gospel with others.

I also come to You with a new impetus and determination to verbally and publicly give You thanks and praise when I pray with others.

*"And being assembled together with them, He commanded them not to depart from Jerusalem, but to wait for the Promise of the Father, "which," He said, "you have heard from Me; for John truly baptized with water, but **you shall be baptized with the Holy Spirit** not many days from now..."*

*... But you shall **receive power when the Holy Spirit has come upon you**; and you shall be witnesses to Me in Jerusalem, and in all Judea and Samaria, and to the end of the earth."*

Acts 1:4-8

DAY 20

Seek the Giver and Not Just the Gift!

One Sunday morning at church, we had a guest speaker and the subject he spoke about was—

"Seek the Giver …not just the Gift!"

I was challenged the moment I heard him speak those words and then he followed on by saying-

"What is the greater; the gift or the giver of that gift?"

Obviously, the giver of the gift is the greater! I knew that God wants us to ask Him for things and that we should earnestly seek the best spiritual gifts. The Bible is full of examples where God requires us to ask of Him in order to receive and be full, yet this was different. The speaker did not say *not* to ask God for anything, only to seek the Giver more.

I thought to myself,

"When was the last time I prayed to God without asking Him for the usual requests but instead sought Him for Who He is and not just for what I could receive!?"

This became a turning point in my spiritual life and relationship with God.

I had been a Christian for over forty years at that time. I had done much service and ministry; held office as a Sunday school superintendent, deacon and elder but … God was calling me to come even closer to Him. I needed it! He did not desire me to do more "service" or have some special "calling" to do a work but rather to seek Him alone for myself. After the service had ended, I left quite excited facing a venture that was going to be new to me!

That evening, I picked up my Bible, and went into a quiet room closing the door behind me and spent a good while in God's presence. After reading the Psalms for a while, I placed my Bible down and got on my knees to pray. I even told myself to be quiet and focus my mind upon God and His Word.

I thought of that Scripture that says-

> *"Be still and know that I am God"*
> **Psalm 46:10**

I began to thank God for His Salvation in Jesus and for saving a sinner like me. I thanked Him for His Word and continued in that manner for a long while. It was good! I felt the presence of the Spirit with me all the way.

I recalled that the psalmist spoke much about receiving God's attributes for himself, things that I really ever heard prayed for — so I began to pray in a similar fashion:

> *Teach me Your Word;*
> *Fill me with Your love;*
> *Show me Your paths that I might walk in them;*
> *Teach me Your ways;*
> *I desire to be like You.*

By praying in this more intimate, open and personal fashion on a regular basis, it became clear over time that changes were taking place, changes that I had not particularly asked for or even thought about but God gave me them anyway! It was as though God was downloading into my heart something of His nature and qualities, things that a person could never imitate or achieve by themselves.

For example, whilst God hates our sin God loves the sinner. That is, He loves people and my love increased so that every person I saw became special. As a result, I found it easier and more natural to talk to people and share with them my testimony about the wonderful news of the Gospel.

Compassion increased as did my faith and trust in the Living God. His presence became more of a reality every day. I became less afraid and anxious about the many problems that face us all in the world and in day to day life. In short, God was much more real to me and I began serving Him in a new and different way. It is never ending to learn of God so the list is ongoing. Just as the Bible says, we are being changed from glory unto glory!

Primarily, this is what my book is all about— *"Living in His Presence"* from day to day and consequently, being changed from within by God. The Lord loves us and desires us, through our submission to Him, to experience His love towards us in Christ Jesus so that, as a result, we can share His Word with others in an authentic manner.

THOUGHT

"Eye has not seen, nor ear heard,
Nor have entered into the heart of man
The things which God has
prepared for those who love Him
But God has revealed them to us through
His Spirit.
For the Spirit searches all things, yes,
The deep things of God…"
1 Corinthians 2:9-10

MEDITATION

Paul, the Apostle, once said —

*"…that **I may know Him** and the power of His resurrection…"*
Philippians 3:10

DAY 21

Abiding in Christ

Probably the most important and profound passage in the Bible regarding the need—the command—to draw close to God are the words of Jesus when He said:

> "I am the true vine, and My Father is the vinedresser. Every branch in Me that does not bear fruit He takes away; and every branch that bears fruit He prunes, that it may bear more fruit. You are already clean because of the word which I have spoken to you. **Abide in Me, and I in you.** As the branch cannot bear fruit of itself, unless it abides in the vine, neither can you, unless you abide in Me.
>
> I am the vine; you are the branches. **He who abides in Me, and I in him, bears much fruit;** for without Me you can do nothing. If anyone does not abide in Me, he is cast out as a branch and is withered; and they gather them and throw them into the fire, and they are burned. **If you abide in Me, and My words abide in you, you will ask what you desire, and it shall be done for you.** By this My Father is glorified, that you bear much fruit; so, you will be My disciples.
>
> As the Father loved Me, I also have loved you; abide in My love. If you keep My commandments, you will abide in My love, just as I have kept My Father's commandments and abide in His love.

> *These things I have spoken to you, that My joy may remain in you, and that your joy may be full."*
>
> **John 15:1-11**

The word "abide" means *to stay, continue, dwell* and *remain*. Jesus likens Himself to vine and likens us to the branches. Since the branch is dependent on the vine for its life-support, so, spiritually, we need the life of Christ in us if we are to be fruitful. God's desire is that we bear much fruit. The Father does the pruning so that this becomes possible, in a similar way to a gardener who prunes his rose bushes to obtain more abundant, healthy roses.

Thought

What does "to prune" mean to each one of us spiritually? This is essentially the message here but there are other points that Jesus is making that we all need to address by choosing to do as He commands.

So far, we have put our faith and trust in Jesus; we are "in Christ" as born-again believers but this passage declares something quite different! Jesus commands us to dwell and remain in Him, and it is our choice whether to do so or not! This is significant because our spiritual life and growth depicted here as life flowing from Jesus into us just as the sap flows from the vine into the branch. The only way, therefore, to grow and mature in Christ spiritually is to come and abide in Him and hence maintain this spiritual flow from Jesus into our life. Without Him, we can do nothing! So, if a person does not abide in Jesus the passage says they are cast out as a branch and thrown into the fire and they are burned! The branch can only dry up, wither and die when no life flows through it.

Further, Jesus tells us that if we abide in Him and His Word abides in us, then we can ask what we desire, and it shall be done! This means that our praying and asking will take on a new dimension.

> *"If you abide in Me, and My words abide in you, you will ask what you desire, and it shall be done for you."*
>
> **John 15:7**

If a branch is cut off a grape vine, then sap is visibly seen flowing out of the cut. This, of course, is the life, the sustaining energy that gives life to the branch and causes it to bud, flower and then bring forth its fruit. This illustration serves as a vivid image pointing to what happens to us spiritually as we abide in Him!

Believe that when you come to Christ in your private prayers and when you are receiving and taking to heart all of His Word, you are connected to Him just as He has illustrated. By the Holy Spirit, you can draw upon His strength and help in time of need! As you believe, you will receive.

Allow the Holy Spirit to come to you; open up your heart in prayer and praise Jesus! Let miracles happen in your life! Jesus has declared the reason He is telling us these things:

> *"These things I have spoken to you, that My joy may remain in you, and that your joy may be full!"*
>
> **John 15:11**

Do you now understand the purposes of abiding in him and allowing His presence and word to abide in us?

It is that we may bring forth fruit and grow to be abundantly fruitful.

- That our praying and asking can become more effective.

- That we glorify God with our fruit bearing and demonstrate our discipleship to Jesus.

- That our joy becomes full through experiencing Christ's own joy!

THOUGHTS & PRAYER

How often I have gone through trials and difficult situations, O Lord, and yet You have seen me through, and I have felt much better afterwards!
   Upon looking back, perhaps You have been "pruning" me, so that I can bear much more fruit and be more like You.
   I now realise that sanctification, testing and pruning are all part of growing up spiritually and that I need not fear it, because it is You doing the work in me and not some enemy.
   O Lord, I desire to embrace all of Your Words by taking them to heart. Fill me O Lord with Your Holy Spirit that I may increase in prayer, praise and worship as well as giving of thanks so that —
   "My joy may be full!"

DAY 22

The Secret Place

Jesus said:

> "But you, when you pray, go into your room and when you have shut the door, pray to your Father who is in the **secret place**; and your Father who sees in secret will reward you openly."
> **Matthew 6:6**

There are many verses in the Bible that refer to seeking God in an intimate way, but nothing can supersede what it means to abide in Christ and dwell in the Secret Place! For example, we are told many times to seek God; to wait upon God; to call upon God and so on, but the ultimate communion that embraces all of these is to abide in Christ!

"The Secret Place" is a common phrase and for the purpose of this book, we shall define it as drawing near to and abiding in Christ. In the passage above, Jesus calls it by this name but most other references to the *Secret Place* are found in the Old Testament.

The context of this verse is not Jesus criticizing public prayer but rather when He says, "go into your room when you pray and shut the door," He is condemning showy, pretentious, attention seeking prayer. Jesus is stressing the importance of coming to our Father into that holy place of private, personal communion with God by entering into the Holy of Holies! This special "secret place" should be the essence of our personal prayer life and will enable us to see growth in our character.

We would do well, right from the start, to recognise the immense importance of entering *the secret place* and abiding in Christ. It is the place where things get done!

> *"He who abides in the **secret place** of the Most High*
> *Shall abide under the shadow of the Almighty"*
> **Psalm 91:1**

In this verse, the word "secret" is very full of meaning! It comes from a word that means "a cover" and can be described as the following:

- *A hiding place;*

- *A place of protection;*

- *To keep close and hide by covering.*[4]

They who abide in the secret place of the Most High abide **under His Shadow!**

How welcome shade can be when walking in the countryside on a hot summer's day! It is a place of immediate relief and refuge from the scorching heat of the sun! God desires us to shelter in Him especially when the road we are travelling on gets tough.

In the passage above, the word "secret" is referring to "a place" but in the following verse, it is different; here it refers to interaction with a person.

---

[4] *Strong's Concordance,* ©1980 by James Strong, Madison, NJ

*"The **secret** of the Lord is with those who fear Him, and He will show them His covenant."*
Psalm 25:14

The word "secret" in this verse means:

- *A company of persons in close deliberation;*

- *Counsel*[5]

God reveals His secret counsel in close friendship just as He did with His disciples. Jesus said to His disciples:

"You are My friends if you do whatever I command you. No longer do I call you servants, for a servant does not know what his master is doing; but I have called you friends, for all things that I heard from My Father I have made known to you."
John 15:14-15

We need God's counsel! He gives us wisdom, guidance and a sense of spiritual understanding and direction. According to this verse, together with Psalm 25: 14, God promises to make known all that the Father has said to His obedient children as they draw in close to Him. He will reveal to us "His covenant", His promises, His Word and His counsel.

---

[5] *Strong's Concordance, ©1980 by James Strong, Madison, NJ*

PRAYER

I come to seek You, O Lord, for Who You are.
I desire to know You more and learn from You.
I thank You for inviting me to come to You.
Forgive me when I have failed to do so in the past.

DAY 23

The Fear of the Lord

The reader will notice how often we look at verses of Scripture from the Psalms and the book of Proverbs where "the fear of the Lord" is mentioned frequently. However, it was Jesus Who said—

> *"And do not fear those who kill the body but cannot kill the soul. But rather **fear Him** who is able to destroy both soul and body in hell."*
> **Matthew 10:28**

There are many examples in Scripture regarding the fear of the Lord; here are some:

> ***"The fear of the Lord** is the beginning of wisdom, And the knowledge of the Holy One is understanding."*
> **Proverbs 9:10**

> *"The secret of the Lord is with those who **fear Him**, And He will show them His covenant."*
> **Psalm 25:14**

(Also see Psalm 112: 1; Proverbs 3:7)

This repetition implies that "the fear of the Lord" is very important—but what does it mean? Why is it mentioned so many times?

The word "fear" in the context above means "reverence" as opposed to terror or panic. This, in turn, means to have *respect, awe* and *devotion*. These qualities are of paramount importance and clarify our actual standing in God's eyes.

For example, if I have a fear to disobey the Lord, then this is a healthy fear! I will eschew evil. I will always desire his ways and follow His will and never seek to do my own thing. I will honour Him everywhere I go and never be ashamed of Him.

The Psalmist declares:

*Behold, the eye of the Lord is on those **who fear Him**,*
On those who hope in His mercy.
Psalm 33:18

The Lord sees and knows those who fear Him; those who will respect and trust Him. Such people also keep His Word in their hearts and reverently obey Him.

My Personal Experience

When I came to the Lord, I heard God speak to my heart and knew it was Him speaking! This reality of God's presence brought a sense of awe within me that I could never forget. Something was ingrained, rooted and fixed within my inner being and it was this—God is real. He is a living person. He knows and sees me, and I can never hide anything from Him whether in thought, word or deed. He is there! He knows every thought; He sees every action!

God's Word had been spoken to me in strong influential words, and once again I could never forget them! Their influence guided my life thereafter. I feared to disobey God or move out of His will with every decision right from the very beginning; that was it! I simply did not desire to displease Him. Every choice was preceded by thinking—

"What would the Lord have me do?"

I felt like I was no longer walking alone in life; now there were two of us and I felt accountable to God. When I became married, then there were three of us because my wife and I equally feared the Lord and desired only to do His will for our life together.

I remember my wife having a completely different experience to that of myself when she came to the Lord. The Word that spoke to her was that the Lord had loved her with an everlasting love and with loving kindness He had drawn her to Himself!

"The Lord has appeared of old to me, saying: "Yes, I have loved you with an everlasting love; Therefore, with lovingkindness I have drawn you."
Jeremiah 31:3

She had been drawn by the fact that God loved her! Thereafter, we both had to make our own individual choices. Sometimes choices and decisions affected both of us together. Either way, we both followed the Lord seeking to do His will as husband and wife as well as individuals, for we all must give a personal account of ourselves to God.

Obedience was the real key that opened doors. Through this, we were actually making God Lord over our lives. We do well to always remember — God is for us and not against us! When I learned to totally trust that the Lord knew what was best for me, even more than I knew myself, then I could yield unconditionally to Him and accept His leading as the right way for me in faith.

One day when I was reading the Bible, I came across a verse that really stood out to me. It was this:

"Every word of God is pure; He is a shield to those who put their trust in Him."
Proverbs 30:5

This showed me that God always had the very best in mind for my life even when the Word may have seemed tough. God's Word always declares what is the most healthy, peaceful and happy way for me to go. He is a shield of protection as I obey Him. If I depart from any part of His Word or ignore it, I will miss out. Now God does not punish us for doing so — not at all! However, in the area of my life where I do not yield to His Word, His shield of protection is absent!

It was the fear of the Lord that sensitised both of our decision making so that the only road my wife and I could walk upon was the one chosen by God. If I desire a close walk with God, if I desire God to speak to me continually guiding my every decision, then there is a condition — live by His Word as it is written!

"Can two walk together except they be agreed?"
Amos 3:3

Remember, coming to God daily and living in His presence is the secret to cultivating a real living relationship with Him. The greatest path to take in life is to walk with the Lord and be kept by His grace. By seeking God and coming to Him, you will become familiar with His voice and know His love all the days of your life!

Jesus said:

"I am the good shepherd; and I know My sheep, and am known by My own. My sheep hear My voice, and I know them, and they follow Me"
John 10:14, 27

THOUGHT & MEDITATION

"…grow in the Grace and knowledge of our Lord and Saviour Jesus Christ."
2 Peter 3:18

DAY 24

The Secret Place — God Our Refuge

God is our refuge and strength,
A very present help in trouble.
Therefore, we will not fear,
Psalm 46:1-2

We all need to rest awhile at times, and God declares Himself as our **refuge** and strength!

There was a time when God's people became weary through trekking the wilderness, so He brought them to a place called "Elim." Here they found twelve wells of water and seventy palm trees and they camped there by the waters. (See Exodus 15:27) He had brought them to a place of refuge and rest.

"Come to Me," said Jesus, "All you who labour and are heavy laden and I will give you rest!"
Matthew 11:28

How welcoming it is to have a God and Saviour Who welcomes us into His intimate presence and company that He might bless and strengthen us! Jesus went on to say,

"Take My yoke upon you and learn from Me, for I am gentle and lowly in heart and you will find rest for your souls."
Matthew 11:28-29

No matter how downtrodden we may feel, Jesus has declared Himself as our place of sanctuary!

The first attribute of the secret place is that it is a place of refuge and rest! We hide in Him, our rock and place of safety, and shelter under "His wings."

> *"For this cause everyone who is godly shall pray to You in a time when You may be found;*
> *Surely in a flood of great waters*
> *They shall not come near him.*
> ***You are my hiding place;***
> ***You*** *shall preserve me from trouble;*
> ***You*** *shall surround me with songs of deliverance.*
> **Psalm 32:7**

Notice how the Psalmist declares that God Himself does these things —

> *He hides us,*
> *He preserves us,*
> *He gives us songs releasing us into His freedom!*

God is our hiding place! — Think about this!

> *"For in the time of trouble*
> ***He shall hide me*** *in His pavilion;*
> *In the secret place of His tabernacle*
> ***He shall hide me;***
> *He shall set me high upon a rock."*
> **Psalm 27:5**

> *"**You shall hide them in the secret place of Your presence***
> *From the plots of man;*

*You shall keep them secretly in a pavilion
From the strife of tongues."*
                                              Psalm 31:20

We are constantly surrounded by trouble! It can be our trouble; someone else's trouble; the troubles at work; the troubles that are in society or in the world — there is never a shortage of trouble. Job understood something about life when he declared,

"Man, who is born of woman, is of few days and full of trouble!"
                                                   Job 14:1

Troubling times and seasons come and go like weather seasons in nature. The most vital provision of God, especially in such times, is to enter through His opened door to that place of refuge in the secret place where we can abide in His presence. In entering, we will discover many other things besides a place of refuge!

*"The eternal God is **your refuge**, and underneath are the everlasting arms;"*
                                         Deuteronomy 33:27

LYRICS FROM A FAMOUS HYMN

There is a place of quiet rest,
Near to the heart of God,
A place where sin cannot molest,
Near to the heart of God.

O Jesus, blest Redeemer,
Sent from the heart of God,
Hold us, who wait before Thee,
Near to the heart of God.

Cleland Boyd McAfee (1866-1944)

PRAYER

I thank You, Father, that You call me into Your presence! Here I can dwell and think about Your goodness and grace towards me. You give me the help and understanding I need without me even having to ask for it. Today I thank You for being my place of refuge and hiding place!

THOUGHT & MEDITATION

In my book, Living Victoriously in the Last Days, *I emphasize seeking a personal relationship with God – above ALL other things!*

"…because iniquity shall abound, the love of many shall wax cold."
Matthew 24:12

DAY 25

The Secret Place — God Our Strength

The Lord is the strength of my life;
Of whom shall I be afraid?
Psalm 27:1b

Why do we try to do things in our own strength — only to fail — when God has promised to be the strength of our life? God's strength is strength! It imparts boldness, confidence, power and might but we need to appropriate it by our faith and trust in Him. God requires us to believe Him — believe His promises, believe His Word. The moment we choose to do so, we activate the power of His Word in our life. Let us step out in faith and He will cover our life with His hand and watch over us.

In the Old Testament, God commanded Joshua as he was about to take over the leadership from Moses and lead the children of Israel into the Promised Land and said to him personally,

> *"Have I not commanded you?* ***Be strong*** *and of good courage; do not be afraid, nor be dismayed, for the Lord Your God is with you wherever you go."*
> **Joshua 1:9**

God was encouraging Joshua to be strong and not to be fearful or anxious about what lay ahead concerning his future tasks. God assured him, by a guarantee, that He would be with him wherever he would go. In other words, God would not allow Joshua to sink or fail!

Notice, however, that God was telling or rather commanding Joshua to be strong. In response, Joshua would have known that he had to "gird up the loins of his mind" (1 Peter 1:13) and take a grip of the situation but above all, to accept God's directive to him.

God knew what lay ahead and further, Joshua had seen for himself how rebellious and disobedient the children of Israel had been under Moses. A formidable task lay ahead, but God, knowing Joshua's heart, saw that he was up to it and that he would indeed trust and obey Him. He was one of the two men who gave a good report after spying out the land of Canaan.

Joshua was a great leader and a man of faith, but he needed to be reassured and strengthened by God. He needed this — and so do we! It is foolhardy to think that we can go it alone! When facing a difficult situation, we can perhaps pray in the following manner:

"Lord I really need You! I need Your help this day! Please guide and strengthen me by Your Holy Spirit within and go before me!"

This is why it is so important to seek God and His help and strength. It is within the quiet place of communion with God that we consolidate our faith and trust in Him. Yes, God declares Himself to be our "refuge and strength, a very present help in trouble," (Psalm 46:1) but the reality is that we need to abide in Him in order to appropriate His promise by faith and therefore receive and experience its fulfilment and benefits!

Basically, we are applying a very important Biblical principle here, namely, that all of God's promises are ours "in Christ." Yes, they are ours, but we have to appropriate each one by faith and then we obtain them! (See 2 Corinthians 1:20)

If you like, we proclaim to God and say, "Amen," or "So be it!"

LYRICS FROM A FAMOUS HYMN

There is a place of full release,
Near to the heart of God,
A place where all is joy and peace,
Near to the heart of God.

O Jesus, blest Redeemer,
Sent from the heart of God,
Hold us, who wait before Thee,
Near to the heart of God.

Cleland Boyd McAfee (1866-1944)

MEDITATION

"Finally, my brethren, **be strong in the Lord** *and in the power of His might."*

Ephesians 6:10

PRAYER

Forgive me, Lord, for I have always thought negatively about myself and my own abilities and strength, whenever I have been challenged, instead of believing in Your strength!

Today I ask You to teach me how to pray and believe Your Word for my life! You have promised so many things in Your Word and I'm sure there are promises in Your storehouse waiting for me to enter into.

AMEN – So be it!

DAY 26

The Secret Place — Allowing God to Do His Work

There are so many blessings granted to us if we will come into God's presence to wait upon Him. God can impart virtue into our life including, as we saw yesterday, His strength, through dwelling in the secret place of His presence. Sometimes, without even asking, He gives of His abundance! God loves us to come to Him in person to spend time with Him and when we do, He comes to us!

There is, however, a pre-requisite if we really intend to do business with the Lord and it is this — we will regularly need to spend time in His Word. The Holy Spirit desires to impart into us the life-giving Word of God. Jesus Himself is called the eternal Word so that we can think of it as being about a Person!

"He (Jesus) was clothed with a robe dipped in blood, and His name is called The Word of God."
Revelation 19:13

"In the beginning was the Word, and the Word was with God, and the Word was God... And the Word became flesh and dwelt among us, and we beheld His glory, the glory as of the only begotten of the Father, full of grace and truth."
John 1:1,14

In Scripture, it is clearly understood that Jesus is the personification of the written and spoken word, hence — *"the word became flesh and dwelt among us."*

Being familiar with God's Word enables the Holy Spirit to bring to our remembrance all the truths that are spiritually embedded within it. Further, the Holy Spirit can impart understanding to the Word that we have read whilst waiting upon God. Rarely, if ever, can we fully understand and appreciate everything that the Word of God contains no matter how many commentaries we might read! Deeply embedded within it are the very thoughts, wisdom and counsel of God!

> *"If you seek her as silver,*
> *And search for her as for **hidden treasures**;*
> *Then you will understand the fear of the Lord,*
> *And **find the knowledge of God**.*
> *For **the Lord gives wisdom**;*
> *From His mouth come knowledge and understanding;"*
>
> **Proverbs 2:4-7**

As indicated above, we find that God Himself can impart such treasures by seeking Him as a Person. He can apply familiar Scriptures to our heart with meaning and applications that we have never seen before.

Remember, Jesus said I am the Way, the TRUTH and the Life, therefore the more familiar we are with God's Word, the more the Holy Spirit can commune with us in counsel and in truth revealing to us the person of Jesus Christ.

Consider an ardent athlete who desires to run a faster time, so he practises running every day. Over time, he improves his performance but simultaneously his strength and stamina are also increased. Now he can better sustain the physical endurance through having obtained greater resilience and fitness! In fact, his overall form is improved for the better in many ways. By seeking to remedy one specific thing, namely his timing in running the race, he has simultaneously helped himself in other ways too.

Coming to God in steadfast prayer is very similar. As we enter His living presence and spiritual realm, we will undoubtedly receive far more than what we expected! Basically, we are allowing God to do His work in our life.

What I am about to speak of next relates to my own personal experience in seeking God and reveals how God blesses abundantly, above all that we can ask or think! (Ephesians 3:20)

My Personal Experience

There came a time in my life when I desired to seek God, having been challenged to seek the Giver and not just the gift!

One evening, as mentioned previously, (See Day 16) I picked up my Bible and went into a quiet room, closing the door behind me, and spent a good while in God's presence. After reading from the Psalms, I placed my Bible down and got on my knees to pray. I even told myself to be quiet and focus my mind upon God and His Word! I began to thank God for His Salvation in Jesus. I thanked Him for His Word and continued in that manner for a long while. It was good! I felt the growing presence of the Spirit with me all the way. This was to be the beginning of regular systematic prayer each day. It was a prayer time where I would be primarily focusing upon knowing God as a Person.

Praying in this more intimate, open, personal

fashion on a regular basis became my habit over several months and it became clear that changes were taking place over time, changes that I had not particularly thought about or asked for but which God gave me anyway! I felt different!

First, I was much more at peace in daily life so that problems, which were still there, did not seem to weigh me down as they had done previously! It was like God was downloading into my heart something of His person so that He became far bigger than the problems themselves. God gave me a greater awareness of His presence throughout each day. I became more confident and secure in God knowing that He was always with me and I could pray to Him more easily. My faith increased; my love for God and people also grew.

It was during this period that a new thing took place. God brought me into a new season with Him and it transformed every avenue of my life. This came about entirely as a result of dwelling in His presence.

Essentially, it was this — I had learned something of what it meant to —

Live in His Presence!

MEDITATION

*"Blessed be the God and Father of our Lord Jesus Christ, who has **blessed us with every spiritual blessing** in the heavenly places in Christ."*

Ephesians 1:3

"And you will seek Me and find Me, when you search for Me with all your heart."

Jeremiah 29:13

DAY 27

The Emmaus Road

Setting the scene:

It is only three days since Jesus was crucified. Two disciples of Jesus, one who is called Cleopas, are journeying from Jerusalem to a village called Emmaus about seven miles away. Their countenances are sad and dejected because of recent events. Suddenly, as they are walking along the dusty road, Jesus Himself comes alongside them and walks with them. However, their eyes were restrained so that they did not know Him. This is what follows —

"What kind of conversation is this that you have with one another as you walk and are sad?" asked Jesus.

Cleopas answered and said to Him,
"Are You the only stranger in Jerusalem, and have You not known the things which happened there in these days?"

"What things?" asked Jesus

They said to Him,

"The things concerning Jesus of Nazareth, who was a Prophet mighty in deed and word before God and all the people, and how the chief priests and our rulers delivered Him to be condemned to death, and crucified Him. But we were hoping that it was He who

was going to redeem Israel. Indeed, besides all this, today is the third day since these things happened. Yes, and certain women of our company, who arrived at the tomb early, astonished us. When they did not find His body, they came saying that they had also seen a vision of angels who said He was alive. And certain of those who were with us went to the tomb and found it just as the women had said; but Him they did not see."

Then Jesus said to them,

"O foolish ones, and slow of heart to believe in all that the prophets have spoken! Ought not the Christ to have suffered these things and to enter into His glory?"

Beginning at Moses and all the Prophets, He expounded to them in all the Scriptures the things concerning Himself. Then they drew near to the village where they were going, and He indicated that He would have gone farther. But they constrained Him, saying,

"Abide with us, for it is toward evening, and the day is far spent."

Jesus went in to stay with them. Now it came to pass, as He sat at the table with them, that He took bread, blessed and broke it, and gave it to them. Then their eyes were opened and they knew Him; and He vanished from their sight. And they said to one another,

"Did not our heart burn within us while He

talked with us on the road, and while He opened the Scriptures to us?"

So, they rose up that very hour and returned to Jerusalem, and found the eleven and those who were with them gathered together, saying,

"The Lord is risen indeed, and has appeared to Simon!"

And they told about the things that had happened on the road, and how He was known to them in the breaking of bread.
(See Luke 24:13-35)

Directly after this event, just as Cleopas and his companion were informing the eleven disciples about their experience on the Emmaus road, Jesus Himself stood in the midst of them and greeted them (see Luke 24: 36-49).

Here we read a second time that Jesus opened their understanding that they might comprehend the Scriptures.

The above is an enlightening account of two disciples of Jesus and their encounter with the risen Saviour. It reveals much about the person and nature of God Himself and how He cares for each one of us when in distress or dismay. It also tells us how we all need Jesus to draw alongside us and open our eyes to understand the Scriptures!

Jesus had been acknowledged as many things in the eyes of His disciples and all the people. Upon one occasion in Caesarea Philippi, Jesus asked His disciples a question:

> *"When Jesus came into the region of Caesarea Philippi, He asked His disciples, saying, "Who do men say that I, the Son of Man, am?" So, they said, "Some say John the Baptist, some Elijah, and others Jeremiah or one of the prophets."* He said to them, *"But who do you say that I am?" Simon Peter answered and said, "You are the Christ, the Son of the living God." Jesus answered and said to him, "Blessed are you, Simon Bar-Jonah, for flesh and blood has not revealed this to you, but My Father who is in heaven."*
>
> **Matthew 16:13-17**

This question was probably of special interest to Jesus as He stood in a region where different gods were in abundance. Caesarea Philippi was an ancient Roman city located at the south western base of Mount Hermon. It was adjacent to a spring and related shrine dedicated to the Greek god Pan.

In response to the question Jesus posed to His disciples, we see that it is only by the understanding and illumination imparted by the Holy Spirit that we can realise the true nature and person of Jesus Christ.

"You are the Christ, the Son of the living God."

"Blessed are you, Simon Bar-Jonah, for flesh and blood has not revealed this to you, but My Father who is in heaven."

Let this, together with the story of the two men on the Emmaus road, serve as a reminder to us that it is only possible to understand the Scriptures by the Holy Spirit! They were written under the inspiration of the Spirit of God and therefore we need Him to enlighten the Word to us.

We are told to read the Word of God, study it, research it, meditate upon it, think it and speak it, yet academic excellence is not a requirement in order to do so! God desires His Word to be available to all people and this has been achieved through a person—Jesus Christ.

Anyone can understand the things of God as they come to Him through Christ, because they are spiritually discerned.

> *"And I, brethren, when I came to you, did not come with excellence of speech or of wisdom declaring to you the testimony of God. For I determined not to know anything among you except Jesus Christ and Him crucified.*
>
> *...And my speech and my preaching were not with persuasive words of human wisdom, but in demonstration of the Spirit and of power, that your faith should not be in the wisdom of men but in the power of God.*
>
> *...**no one knows the things of God except the Spirit of God. Now we have received, not the spirit of the world, but the Spirit who is from God, that we might know the things that have been freely given to us by God.**"*
>
> **1 Corinthians 2:1-2, 4-5, 11-12**

A Testimony

When I gave my life to the Lord at the age of nineteen, I looked to God for understanding as I had little or no religious background. This was just as well, in my case!

The verses above were very special to me! They gave me hope that I was able to grasp the things of God as it was not based upon my human intellect and reasoning but upon God Himself!

I was even more pleased and encouraged when I read the following words …

> *"Where is the wise? Where is the scribe? Where is the disputer of this age? Has not God made foolish the wisdom of this world? For since, in the wisdom of God, the world through wisdom did not know God it pleased God through the foolishness of the message preached to save those who believe*
>
> *…For you see your calling, brethren, that not many wise according to the flesh, not many mighty, not many noble, are called. But God has chosen the foolish things of the world to put to shame the wise, and God has chosen the weak things of the world to put to shame the things which are mighty; and the base things of the world and the things which are despised God has chosen, and the things which are not, to bring to nothing the things that are, that no flesh should glory in His presence."*
> **1 Corinthians 1:20-29**

PRAYER

Thank You, Lord Jesus, for the way You care about each one of us especially when we are hurting, in spite of what we might think.

I thank You for the way You came to two of Your disciples and had fellowship with them and spoke personally with them!

I ask You today to lead me into deeper fellowship with You that I might understand the Scriptures too!

You have forgiven me; You have given me Your Holy Spirit! I come now to do my part, that is, to dedicate myself to You by reading Your Word, studying it and learning of YOU!

Amen

DAY 28

Counsel and Understanding

In yesterday's account of the two men on the Emmaus road, it is interesting that it was the second time Jesus after His resurrection seemingly went out of His way to minister to some of His disciples when they were in distress or dismay. The first account was when He appeared unto Mary Magdalene as she stood outside the empty tomb weeping.

Here is the passage taken from John 20:

"As she wept, Mary stooped down and looked into the tomb. And she saw two angels in white sitting, one at the head and the other at the feet, where the body of Jesus had lain. Then they said to her,

"Woman, why are you weeping?"

She said to them,

"Because they have taken away my Lord, and I do not know where they have laid Him."

Now when she had said this, she turned around and saw Jesus standing there, and did not know that it was Jesus. Jesus said to her,

"Woman, why are you weeping? Whom are you seeking?"

> She, supposing Him to be the gardener, said to Him,
> "Sir, if You have carried Him away, tell me where You have laid Him, and I will take Him away."
>
> Jesus said to her,
> "Mary!"
>
> She turned and said to Him,
> "Rabboni!" (which is to say, Teacher)."

Once again, Jesus was not initially recognised by Mary. The purpose of His visit was to reassure Mary in her sorrow and being now risen from the dead, this He did!

Now that Jesus is risen and alive for ever more, seated at the right hand of the Father in Heaven, we can rest assured that, just as with Cleopas and his friend and with Mary Magdalene, He can come to each one of us, His children, and indeed reassure us too!

This has been achieved through the sending of the Holy Spirit. Jesus had previously promised that He would "come to His disciples" in John 14:15-19—

> "If you love Me, keep My commandments. And **I will pray the Father, and He will give you another Helper, that He may abide with you forever—the Spirit of truth,** whom the world cannot receive, because it neither sees Him nor knows Him; but you know Him, for He dwells with you and will be in you. I will not leave you orphans; **I will come to you.**"

We should remember that because all Scripture is inspired by God; we completely depend upon God, the Holy Spirit, to illuminate our minds in order to understand the Scriptures. Just like the disciples of Jesus needed to be shown even though they had lived with Him for several years and got to know Him personally.

In the previous day's readings, much was said regarding the matter of "understanding" the Scriptures through the function and work of the Holy Spirit as the Spirit of Truth.

We also looked at a way to receive a different kind of "understanding" or counsel.

(As seen on Days 21-22 examining *The Secret Place* and *The Fear of the Lord*.)

> *"The fear of the Lord is **the beginning of wisdom, And the knowledge of the Holy One is understanding.**"*
> **Proverbs 9:10**

"The fear of the Lord" by itself, brings about wisdom, knowledge and understanding part of which we may call counsel. God gives me His counsel when I am willing to listen to Him and obey Him. The fear of the Lord is a pre-requisite to understanding! It is all to do with my willingness to receive advice, perspective, instruction and act upon it. This personal deliberation is the key to spiritual maturity and knowing God personally in our life.

> *"The **secret of the Lord** is with those who fear Him, And **He will show them** His covenant."*
> **Psalm 25:14**

This verse clearly states that God will impart His Word with counsel and understanding to those who will abide in the secret place of His presence. Remember this is the same place Jesus told us to go to when praying to the Father. (Matthew 6:6)

We always need to remember that God tells us what is necessary for us know and no more. It would not be expedient for us to know everything! God requires our faith in Him to be paramount. We have to trust God when the outcome of situations in our life is unclear.

We learn much through patience and trust. Instant answers do not necessarily help us, but faith in Him that He will always do what is right is still essential!

The Word encourage us to this end by saying:

"And we know that all things work together for good to those who love God, to those who are the called according to His purpose."

Romans 8:28

PART 3

Prayer Is the Battleground

DAY 29

Spiritual Warfare

What has "warfare" got to do with a child of God? If Jesus destroyed the works of the Devil at the cross, then why should we be involved in any form of warfare?

Before we look at these questions, ask yourself this:

Are there problems on the Earth today? Does sin abound? Does evil flourish?

To begin answering these questions we will look at the prayer Jesus interceded for us all to the Father:

> "I do not pray that You should take them out of the world, but that You should keep them from the evil one. They are not of the world, just as I am not of the world. Sanctify them by Your truth. Your word is truth. As You sent Me into the world, I also have sent them into the world."
> **John 17:15-18**

First of all, Jesus said,

"I do not pray that You should take them out of the world, but that You should keep them from the evil one."

The Bible says that Jesus defeated the Devil upon the cross when He shed His blood for the sins of the whole world.

> *"Inasmuch then as the children have partaken of flesh and blood, He Himself likewise shared in the same, that through death He might destroy him who had the power of death, that is, the devil …"*
> **Hebrews 2:14**

Whereas before, mankind needed a Saviour, now God has provided one—His own Son! Jesus, having defeated the enemy, has now become God's gift of salvation to all who will believe in Him.

> *"But God demonstrates His own love toward us, in that while we were still sinners, Christ died for us."*
> **Romans 5:8**

> *"For God so loved the world that He gave His only begotten Son, that whoever believes in Him should not perish but have everlasting life."*
> **John 3:16**

However, man's freewill, his freedom of choice, must accept and receive God's salvation for themselves. This is only achieved through repentance of sin and receiving Christ as both Lord and Saviour.

Jesus referred to the **"the evil one,"** in His prayer and asked that we may be kept from him. He described us and all those who believe as being **"not of this world!"**

My book, *Living Victoriously in the Last Days*, addresses this subject in detail. In short, the kingdoms of this world are under the jurisdiction of Satan and God's children are called to overcome him by the Blood of the Lamb and by their own testimony and faith in the Word of God. Hence, every believer is involved in spiritual warfare in this world.

The Bible says we can resist the Devil and he will flee from us!

> *"Therefore, submit to God. Resist the devil and he will flee from you."*
> **James 4:7**

Whenever we pray to God in the name of Jesus; whenever we affirm verbally that we are going to trust in God's Word then we can be sure that all evil spirits will turn away.

The enemy knows he has been defeated but will roar like a lion sometimes to make us afraid. He will lie and seek to deceive but he cannot harm those who are trusting in God! It is, therefore, of utmost importance to read and know God's Word. In doing so we will know the Truth and therefore be able to stand against all the accusations thrown at us.

The Devil could not defeat Jesus when tempting him in the wilderness because Jesus replied and said:

"Thus, it is written!"

(Matthew 4:1-11, Mark 1:12-13, Luke 4:1-13)

The Devil knew he was unable to act against the authority of the Word of God! It is still impossible today for him to do so even when we ourselves speak it — such is the authority and power of the Word of God! We should ask ourselves:

"Are we just as sure about the authority of God's Word ourselves as demons are?"

A common tactic of the Devil is to accuse us by saying that we are not good enough. It is true; we are not good enough in our own righteousness, but we can assert that it is the blood of Jesus that has paid the price for our sins. Jesus has justified me and made me right and acceptable before a Holy God!

The Word of God says:

"Who shall bring a charge against God's elect? It is God who justifies.
Who is he who condemns? It is Christ who died, and furthermore is also risen…"
Romans 8:33-34

Whenever you quote God's Word and take a stance against any accusation of the enemy, you are "resisting the devil." The Devil is much stronger than we are, but we have been given this weapon and it will always defeat him—the written Word of God called the Sword of the Spirit! Therefore, know it, pray it over all your life's problems and difficulties, and speak it out regularly. Remember, you will never win any battle in your own strength but with God's weapons you cannot fail.

I find it very beneficial to speak out the Word of God at various times during the day! It is both edifying and purifying.

Jesus continued praying to the Father for us and asked the following:

"Sanctify them by Your truth. Your word is truth."
John 17:7

Jesus wants us to be sanctified by the WORD OF GOD and by the SPIRIT OF GOD. We need to read it every day; be taught it; live it! The Holy Spirit will then be able to use the Word by bringing it to our remembrance and give us the victory!

Throughout our life, God will seek to change us through His working within the inner man. It is as we submit and cooperate with patience that God will change our character. We must be humble and allow ourselves to be corrected and taught by Him. Our life will gradually become more like Christ, indeed, the Bible says we are "being changed from glory unto glory."

> *"But we all, with unveiled face, beholding as in a mirror the glory of the Lord, are being transformed into the same image from glory to glory, just as by the Spirit of the Lord."*
> **2 Corinthians 3:18**

The word "sanctify" means to "set apart." This is because we are no longer of this world in the same way as Jesus was not of this world! In reality, we must submit to the washing and cleansing of the Word and the Holy Spirit and the renewing of our minds.
(See Days 11 and 12)

> *"I beseech you therefore, brethren, by the mercies of God, that you present your bodies a living sacrifice, holy, acceptable to God, which is your reasonable service. And do not be conformed to this world, but* **be transformed by the renewing of your mind***, that you may prove what is that good and acceptable and perfect will of God."*
> **Romans 12:1-2**

We were "saved" when we believed on Christ, but we are "being saved" as we yield to the process of sanctification by the Spirit. This process is often absent in people's lives. It is a choice and needs our commitment. In such cases, were the progressive nature of sanctification is absent, the person is not receiving what Jesus prayed for us to receive! They cannot become more Christ like or mature spiritually and at the worst may be included in the category of "believers" of whom Jesus spoke of saying:

> *"Not everyone who says to Me, 'Lord, Lord,' shall enter the Kingdom of heaven, but he who does the will of My Father in heaven. Many will say to Me in that day, 'Lord, Lord, have we not prophesied in Your name, cast out demons in Your name, and done many wonders in Your name?' And then I will declare to them, 'I never knew you; depart from Me, you who practise lawlessness!'"*
> **Matthew 7:21-23**

It is very clear—this world is not our home! Spiritual warfare is a reality.

The real battleground is in the place of PRAYER. and INTERCESSION!

As you pray to God, He will begin to deal with your prayers in accordance with His will and timing.

> *"…praying always with all prayer and supplication in the Spirit."*
> **Ephesians 6:18**

DAY 30

Spiritual Warfare — Who Is the Enemy?

> *"For **we do not wrestle against flesh and blood**, but against principalities, against powers, against the rulers of the darkness of this age, against spiritual hosts of wickedness in the heavenly places."*
> **Ephesians 6:12**

Very often, especially in the West, people do not consider the idea of spiritual warfare. This attitude is not typical of the rest of the world where spiritual activity of an evil nature is publicly witnessed and experienced. This former attitude is typical and indicative of a modern, secular society that does not find it convenient to consider such things and often attributes them to some form of extremist views.

The reason for this is quite simple; the preaching of the Word of God in many churches across the land never entertains such a subject as "Spiritual Warfare" and all too often, passages involving demon possession are put on the "back burner." The Scriptures clearly tell us that:

> *"All Scripture is given by inspiration of God, and is profitable for doctrine, for reproof, for correction, for instruction in righteousness, that the man of God may be complete, thoroughly equipped for every good work."*
> **2 Timothy 3:16-17**

Therefore, who are we to decide which parts of the Word of God we accept and which parts we reject? This is precisely the attitude evil spirits want us to have!

In general, no matter what the subject, if a church deliberately denies parts of the Word of God or rejects them outright, it will inevitably fall away from God's blessing over time and a door will be opened for infiltration of evil and contrary spirits with their own message instead!

In these last days, the Bible says the denying of sound doctrine will increase and men will give heed to seducing spirits! (See *Living Victoriously in the Last Days* by the same author.)

> *"I charge you therefore before God and the Lord Jesus Christ, who will judge the living and the dead at His appearing and His Kingdom:*
> **Preach the word!**
> **Be ready in season and out of season.**
> **Convince, rebuke, exhort, with all longsuffering and teaching.**
> *For the time will come when they will not endure sound doctrine, but according to their own desires …they will heap-up for themselves teachers; and they will turn their ears away from the truth, and be turned aside to fables."*
> **2 Timothy 4:1-4**

> *"Now the Spirit expressly says that in latter times some will depart from the faith,* **giving heed to deceiving spirits and doctrines of demons,** *speaking lies in hypocrisy, having their own conscience seared with a hot iron…"*
> **1 Timothy 4:1-2**

The truth, as always, is in the written Word of God.

The verse of Scripture at the beginning of this morning's reading describes the reality of the evil realm and states that our enemy is not "man" but rather evil spirits.

"We do not wrestle against flesh and blood!"

But against:

- Principalities
- Against powers
- Against the rulers of the darkness of this age
- Against spiritual hosts of wickedness in the heavenly places.

Ephesians 6:12

*"For though we walk in the flesh, **we do not war according to the flesh**. For the weapons of our warfare are not carnal but mighty in God for pulling down strongholds, casting down arguments and every high thing that exalts itself against the knowledge of God, bringing every thought into captivity to the obedience of Christ."*

2 Corinthians 10:3-5

If we turn back to the beginning in the Garden of Eden, we read that both Adam and Eve gave their allegiance to the Serpent and not God! This was achieved when they chose to believe and obey Satan instead of God! Hence, man's new master was none other than the Devil himself! The same has been true in every generation and is the same today. If we openly disbelieve and reject what God says to us personally, we automatically allow Satan dominion over that part of our life! He only has any power when we give it to him!

Jesus, Who has defeated the Devil upon the cross by His own shed blood, can set us free from the bondage of sin inherent in our sinful human nature which we acquired from birth.

By receiving Jesus, we receive the Holy Spirit and become partakers of the Divine Nature. We are conveyed from the Kingdom of darkness into the Kingdom of light! Whilst our carnal human nature will always lust against the Spirit and vice versa, yet He that is in us is far greater than he that is in the world!

This is how we can live victoriously by faith in this present world. Jesus has triumphed over Satan and the grave!

In spite of the presence of sin in a fallen world, in spite of the presence of evil principalities and powers and wickedness in high places that govern and have rule over nations, we are more than conquerors through Him Who loves us and has washed us from sin in His own blood!

> *"Then Jesus said to those Jews who believed in Him,* **"If you abide in My word, you are My disciples indeed. And you shall know the truth, and the truth shall make you free."**
> **…*therefore, if the Son makes you free, you shall be free indeed."***
> **John 8:31, 36**

One of the greatest strengths the Devil has in society is our rejection of God's Word and His laws that once governed our nation. This can be at both a national level and a personal level. The Serpent deceives! He is a liar!

"Has God indeed said?"
Genesis 3:1

His intention was to arouse doubt by diverting Adam and Eve's attention to what "they would be missing." It worked!

Think for a moment about these "lies" sown into the minds of Eve and then Adam and observe whether such lies are prevalent today! For example, have you ever met people who doubt the Word of God? Have you ever met people who think they will be missing out in life? The very same lies spoken so long ago are still very common in the world today. Without God's intervention, without His saving grace in Jesus we would all be beguiled and forever in bondage!

How did the Devil fare when he confronted Jesus in the wilderness to tempt Him? Was he not defeated at every turn by the Word of God?! This is the one we are all dealing with! One who has no power at all against the authority of God's Word—the Sword of the Spirit. Thanks be to God Who gives us the victory through our Lord Jesus Christ!

A command:

"Finally, my brethren, be strong in the Lord and in the power of His might. Put on the whole armour of God, that you may be able to stand against the wiles of the devil.

...Stand therefore, having girded your waist with truth, having put on the breastplate of righteousness, and having shod your feet with the preparation of the gospel of peace; above all, taking the shield of faith with which you will be able to quench all the fiery darts of the wicked one. And take the helmet of salvation, and the sword of the Spirit, which is the word of God; praying always with all prayer and supplication in the Spirit, being watchful to this end with all perseverance and supplication..."
Ephesians 6:10-18

DAY 31

The Heavenly Places

> "He has delivered us from the power of darkness and conveyed (translated) us into the kingdom of the Son of His love"
> **Colossians 1:13**

This is the reality! This our situation in Christ! We are seated in the heavenly places with Him.

The "transference" of the believer from under Satan's authority to Christ's is described as movement into another "Kingdom!" The Bible also calls this being "made alive" from being spiritually dead!

> "And you **He made alive**, who were dead in trespasses and sins, in which you once walked according to the course of this world, according to the prince of the power of the air… "
> **Ephesians 2:1-2**

This passage shows that we were once spiritually dead through sin and separated from God walking in accordance with the will of the "prince of the power of the air."

The very thought of being alienated from God and subject to the evil powers in the "air" seems dreadful indeed and yet, that is exactly how we once were! This is still the case for all those outside of Christ who have never believed in Him.

In this final day of meditations, we are going to see from Scripture that the spiritual world is very active, it is very real; it is all around us and we are part of it.

In the Book of Ephesians, there are many references to what is termed "the Heavenly Places."

> *"...that you may know... what is the exceeding greatness of His power toward us who believe, according to the working of His mighty power which He worked in Christ when He raised Him from the dead and seated Him at His right hand **in the heavenly places**, far above all **principality and power and might and dominion**, and every name that is named..."*
>
> **Ephesians 1:18-21**

Here, we see Christ seated in the "Heavenly Places" at God's right hand. "Heavenly Places" does not so much refer to heaven in the sense of its being the destined home of the redeemed. Rather, the Greek word here refers to the invisible realm that surrounds our present daily situation; the arena or sphere of spiritual action and activity.[6] Christ's authority, which exceeds every known power, is here and now!

The New Testament further reveals an invisible hierarchy of evil powers who deceive and manipulate human behaviour to advance satanic strategies. The terms consistently used for these evil ruling authorities are:

> *"...**Principalities, and power and might and dominion**..."*

---

[6] *Strong's Concordance, ©1980 by James Strong, Madison, NJ*

> *"For we do not wrestle against flesh and blood, but against **principalities, against powers, against the rulers of the darkness of this age, against spiritual hosts of wickedness in the heavenly places.**"*
>
> **Ephesians 6:12**

Christ Himself is placed in authority over all these powers. All who are in Christ are placed in a position of authority together with Him as they exercise spiritual warfare as stated above.

> *"...But God, who is rich in mercy, because of His great love with which He loved us, even when we were dead in trespasses, made us alive **TOGETHER with Christ... and raised us up TOGETHER, and made us sit TOGETHER in the heavenly places in Christ Jesus**..."*
>
> **Ephesians 2:4-6**

The passage above declares how that we also — the redeemed of the Lord — have been:

> *"made alive"* and *"raised up together and made to sit together in the Heavenly Places with Christ!"*

The three "togethers" in verses 5 and 6 show us our union with Christ.

- In His resurrection
- In His ascension
- In His present rule at God's right hand.

From this place of partnership, He grants that we share in the present works of His Kingdom's power even as it is written:

> *"For we are His workmanship,* **created in Christ Jesus for good works***, which God prepared beforehand that we should walk in them."*
> **Ephesians 2:10**

The title of this book is:

'Living in His Presence'

Having been made spiritually alive from the dead in Christ; having been translated from the Kingdom of darkness into the Kingdom of light; having died with Christ in the flesh and risen with Him in the Spirit, we are able to walk in newness of life, living in His presence continuously! Christ is forever with us. Simply to utter His name ushers in the presence of God.

Thus far, God has ***done*** everything, and we have ***received*** everything! What remains is our consecration to Christ as His servants; God now requires loyalty. This world is not our home just as it wasn't with Jesus. Remember how He said to Pilate:

> *"My Kingdom is not of this world!"*
> **John 18:36**

We, the redeemed of the Lord, are members of the very same kingdom that Jesus spoke of—the kingdom of God! To be consecrated therefore to God, I need to be dedicated wholly to God's will for my life serving the interests of the King. In short, I must look at Jesus and the way He walked upon this earth—then do likewise! (See DAY 6.)

> *"I beseech you therefore, brethren, by the mercies of God, that ye **present your bodies a living sacrifice**, holy, acceptable unto God, which is your reasonable service. And be not conformed to this world: but be ye transformed by the renewing of your mind, that ye may prove what is that good, and acceptable, and perfect, will of God."*
> **Romans 12:1-2**

I need to recognise that I am not my own, I have been purchased (redeemed) by the blood of Jesus. I now belong to Christ as His purchased possession! In other words, I am a bondservant or a slave.

> *"Or do you not know that your body is the temple of the Holy Spirit who is in you, whom you have from God, and **you are not your own? For you were bought at a price;** therefore, glorify God in your body and in your spirit, which are God's."*
> **1 Corinthians 6:19-20**

Will you humble yourself, take this challenge and be a servant of Christ in the truest sense?

Many years ago, I spoke to a group of mostly young people and gave them a practical demonstration showing the length of each of our lives. I simply took a piece of string and hung it vertically. I then set it alight at its end and when the flame was large enough, I extinguished it. All that could be seen was smoke ascending into the air and vanishing away.

"This is your life," I said and then read out two Scriptures from my Bible:

"... For what is your life?
It is even a vapour that appears for a little time and then vanishes away."
James 4:14

"... And the world is passing away, and the lust of it; but he who does the will of God abides forever."
1 John 2:17

When I had finished my talk, a young man of about nineteen years of age stood alone after all the others had left and wished to talk with me privately. He had been moved by the Word and asked for prayer. He was in fact, a born-again believer but, nevertheless, wanted to give his life over to the Lord!

God speaks to each one of us personally at appointed times — if we have ears to hear — and so often, He desires more of our life to be given over to Him! He wishes to draw us closer to Himself!

Dear reader, now is the time! Now, whilst it is day, is the opportunity to give our lives to the Lord, for our salvation is closer now than when we first believed. The night comes when no man can work!

As Isaiah the prophet put it-

> *"Seek the Lord while He may be found,*
> *Call upon Him while He is near."*
>
> **Isaiah 55:6**

PRAYER

I thank You, Father, for forgiving me and receiving me into Your Kingdom of Light as Your child through Jesus Christ and His shed blood for me!

I come this day to surrender my all to You, to do Your will and not my own, to seek Your Kingdom first, counting every earthly gain as secondary in comparison to You!

> *Were the whole realm of nature mine,*
> *That were an offering far too small;*
> *Love so amazing, so divine,*
> *Demands my soul, my life, my all.*
>
> **Isaac Watts (1674-1748)**

MY TESTIMONY

At the age of nineteen, I was living at home with my parents in a place called Langwith Junction in Derbyshire, England, which, as the name suggests, was a railway junction with sheds full of steam engines. It was a small village about one mile away from Shirebrook, a coal-mining market town.

By now I was well into university studies at Chelsea College of Science, London, and I always looked forward to coming home during vacation times to see my then girlfriend, Pauline Marchant, who lived about seven miles away in Mansfield. She was awesome, and I considered myself very lucky! It was during one Easter vacation in the year 1966 that I was ill in bed with the flu at my mum's house. I remember feeling quite low. My mother asked me to come to church with her as she said I would feel much better if I did. Being a dark cold Wednesday evening, I reluctantly yielded to her pressure, feeling I had no option but to go. "At least," I thought, "it is dark outside, and no one will particularly see me and where I am going!" You see, I felt stupid and embarrassed going to a church.

Upon arrival at a medium-sized Pentecostal Church Hall in Shirebrook, I saw no one there except two or three very elderly people—my mum had not told me it was a Prayer Meeting! To my utter amazement I recognised the man who stood at the front; it was Archie Roberts, and he owned a Fish and Chip shop in town!

I sat down sheepishly near the front feeling very conspicuous and downcast. Archie read out a verse or two from the Bible and began to preach. He read the passage from Matthew 16: 24-26 which went as follows:

"*Then Jesus said to His disciples, "If anyone desires to come after Me, let him deny himself, and take up his cross, and follow Me. For whoever desires to save his life will lose it, but whoever loses his life for My sake will find it. For what profit is it to a man if he gains the whole world, and loses his own soul? Or what will a man give in exchange for his soul?"*

He talked about man being born into this world naked, with nothing, and leaving it in a similar fashion. I was always inspired by truth, and this I could not dispute — it was true! As he went on about life, the Word began to speak to me — what would it profit me if I were to gain all the riches in the world only to die and then, that's it? I would leave everything behind! As a student I had plans to live a full life, hopefully with a good job, but this Word I was hearing shook me up to think more deeply and seriously. What was the meaning and purpose of my life? Where was I going? What was after?

Being prompted by mum's elbow, I stood up at the end of the meeting to walk out to the front and be prayed for, giving my life to JESUS CHRIST.

I knew something spiritual had taken place that evening in the little hall; in fact, something supernatural! I had walked into the hall not knowing anything about God, but I walked out knowing this…

GOD was VERY REAL; I knew because, somehow, I had just met with HIM! Like I said, something spiritual happened; I don't know how — but it did!

From that day forward to this very day, some fifty-two years later, God has been so real and personal to me. I had once said mockingly to my mum that if God is real then He should talk with us and for that matter we with Him!

I instantly became hungry to read the Bible. I got to know Him more and more through His Word, which was opened up to me by His in-dwelling Holy Spirit!

He gave me what I was looking for — a purpose and reason for life, but most importantly, a real living relationship with God. I was not interested in religion but knowing God for myself — that was very different!

Now, I know this life is not the end but that it goes on with Him FOREVER!

Brian Reddish

BOOKS BY THE SAME AUTHOR

There Is a Balm in Gilead:
God's Healing Love, Grace and Compassion

A collection of 5 Inspiring Short Stories

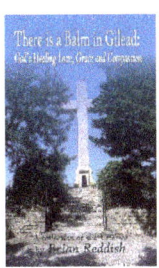

The Dorothy McGuire Series

Dorothy McGuire: Book 1

Beautiful Dorothy McGuire carries a hidden, cruel, dark past – childhood sexual abuse!

Will she ever find release? Will be ever experience a normal relationship?

Dorothy McGuire: Book 2

An exciting continuation from Book 1 about how ordinary people's lives can be touched by an extraordinary God!

Dorothy McGuire:
Book 3 – The Final Chapter

This book brings to an end Dorothy's incredible journey and completes the MUST-READ trilogy!

Living Victoriously in the Last Days

A 31-day devotional

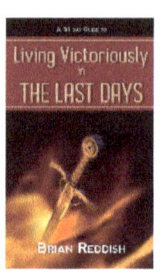

I Found Reality

An Autobiography

All Books available in Print and e-book format.

Published by Caracal Books.

CONTACT THE AUTHOR

www.brianreddishbooks.uk

NOTES

NOTES

NOTES

NOTES

NOTES

NOTES

www.ingramcontent.com/pod-product-compliance
Lightning Source LLC
Chambersburg PA
CBHW042114100526
44587CB00025B/4052